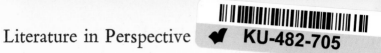

Literature in Perspective

T. S. Eliot

T. S. Pearce

Evans Brothers Limited, London

Published by Evans Brothers Limited
Montague House, Russell Square, London, W.C.1

First published 1967
Reprinted 1969

Set in 11 on 12 pt. Bembo and printed in Great Britain
by The Camelot Press Ltd., London and Southampton

237 44545 x cased
237 44546 8 limp   PR 2405

Literature in Perspective

Reading is a pleasure; reading great literature is a great pleasure, which can be enhanced by increased understanding, both of the actual words on the page and of the background to those words, supplied by a study of the author's life and circumstances. Criticism should try to foster understanding in both aspects.

Unfortunately for the intelligent layman and young reader alike, recent years have seen critics of literature (particularly academic ones) exploring slender ramifications of meaning, exposing successive levels of association and reference, and multiplying the types of ambiguity unto seventy times seven.

But a poet is 'a man speaking to men', and the critic should direct his efforts to explaining not only what the poet says, but also what sort of man the poet is. It is our belief that it is impossible to do the first without doing the second.

LITERATURE IN PERSPECTIVE, therefore, aims at giving a straightforward account of literature and of writers—straightforward both in content and in language. Critical jargon is as far as possible avoided; any terms that must be used are explained simply; and the constant preoccupation of the authors of the Series is to be lucid.

It is our hope that each book will be easily understood, that it will adequately describe its subject without pretentiousness so that the intelligent reader who wants to know about Donne or Keats or Shakespeare will find enough in it to bring him up to date on critical estimates.

Even those who are well read, we believe, can benefit from a lucid expression of what they may have taken for granted, and perhaps—date it be said?—not fully understood.

K. H. G.

T. S. Eliot

In a collection of essays for Eliot's sixtieth birthday, William Empson wrote:

> I feel, like most other verse writers of my generation, that I do not know for certain how much of my own mind he invented, let alone how much of it is a reaction against him or indeed a consequence of misreading him. He has a very penetrating influence, perhaps not unlike an east wind.

Eliot's influence is such that it is impossible to judge 20th-century poetry without coming to terms with his work. It is challenging, because it is mostly experimental, not only in form and style, but also in thought and insight, and the reader who brings expectations of the sort of pleasure provided by the majority of earlier poets will be disappointed. Once the effort is made to approach Eliot's work closely, the reader's whole response to poetry will be enriched.

His poetry is difficult for two reasons, one of which may be overcome, and one which may always be a barrier. He developed new forms and styles which are still startling, and at first off-putting, but not in the end impassable. At the same time he chose to write of complex and difficult themes, near the boundaries of thought, and these will always be hard to understand. You feel that a final comprehension is just round the corner, but it's a corner you never reach.

Although it is not always easy to discover the simple ideas which lie at the base of Eliot's poetry, there is absolutely no question about his sincerity in approaching the central emotional experiences with which he is concerned, and eventually as he himself reaches towards simplicity, the simple ideas on which the complex ones are built up gradually become clear.

6

Contents

The Author

T. S. Pearce, M.A., is English Master at Brighton College.

Acknowledgements

The author and publishers are indebted to *The Times* for permission to reproduce the cover portrait; Mrs. T. S. Eliot for the portrait of her husband at sixteen and for one of his poems; Edwin Snell & Sons, printers, for the photograph of East Coker; *The Birmingham Post* for the one of Burnt Norton and P. G. M. Dickinson, F.S.A., F.R.Hist.S., for the one of the chapel at Little Gidding.

They are also indebted to Faber & Faber Ltd. for permission to quote from the works of T. S. Eliot; to Farrar, Straus & Giroux, Inc. for the USA rights to quote from *The Elder Statesman, On Poetry and Poets*, and *The Possibility of Poetic Drama*, and to Harcourt, Brace & World, Inc. for the USA rights to quote from the rest of Eliot's works. Also to Charles Scribner's Sons for the quotation from *Axel's Castle* by Edmund Wilson; Mr. M. B. Yeats, Macmillan & Co. Ltd. and the Macmillan Company of New York for the extract from *Symbolism in Poetry* by W. B. Yeats published in *Essays and Introductions*; Oxford University Press, Inc. for the extract from *The Achievement of T. S. Eliot* by F. O. Matthiessen, and Frank Cass & Co. Ltd. for the quotation from *The Dramatic Verse of T. S. Eliot* by E. Martin Browne, published in *T. S. Eliot—A Symposium*, edited by Tambimuttu & March (3rd impression, August 1965).

I

Life: 1888–1965

T. S. Eliot was an American. He came to England in 1914 at the age of twenty-six. He worked in a bank and later became a director of an important publishing house. He presented himself in a British manner, with umbrella, striped trousers, and bowler hat. He rejected many of the causes which make up the American tradition, the cause of the emigration to America, of the War of Independence, and of the Civil War. He never returned to America except as a visitor. In 1927, he became a British subject, and a confirmed member of the Church of England. He developed a perfectly standard English accent. He appeared to possess a characteristic English reticence. He liked English cheeses. Nevertheless, none of these things really disguised the fact that he was an American and that in attitude and tradition he fits more easily into the American context than into the British, especially when you remember that to live and work out of America has been characteristic of American writers at all times, and that the search for a 'character' in the absence of any specific and certain American character with which a writer would wish to be associated has also been typical, especially since the decline of the New England culture, and the vast expansion of the United States towards the end of the 19th century. He wore his new nationality, and his English characteristics, rather as a mask, covering, though not exactly hiding, a powerful individual largely detached from such matters as nationality. He was also a European, and that is a title almost as unrevealing as American.

The powerful individual, rejecting any label or classification, is revealed in his poetry. It has little in common with either his English or American contemporaries, though it is closer if anything to the American writers, especially to Ezra Pound. Eliot did not write a great deal, but with the exception of a few minor pieces, each poem is concentrated, intense, and unique. He makes no concessions to his 'audience' who are expected to make a considerable effort to comprehend his work, and he experimented constantly with form and style so that each reader must adjust his preconceived ideas of the nature of poetry at almost every page. His work is difficult mainly because its manner is still unfamiliar and strange, even to the experienced reader, while the ideas he handles are in themselves complex. He is not, however, difficult because of syntactical disorder such as you may find in Milton, or because of compression of imagery such as you may find in Shakespeare. He uses chiefly a standard English conversational idiom, described by himself in *Little Gidding*:

> The common word exact without vulgarity,
> The formal word precise but not pedantic,
> The complete consort dancing together.

He was born on 26th September, 1888, in St. Louis, Missouri, an industrial city in the centre of the United States which had pretensions to become one of the great cities of the nation. He was the son of Henry Eliot and Charlotte Stearns, in whom are combined various qualities which reveal themselves in Eliot's life. His father's family came to America in 1668 from East Coker in Somerset and had become merchants in New England, specifically in Boston, the centre of early American society, and especially the cultural centre of America in the 19th century. His grandfather, however, had left New England for St. Louis in 1834. He was a minister of the Unitarian Church, the branch of Christianity which does not believe in the Trinity, but in a single God only. He established a Unitarian church in St. Louis, and became one of the most important figures in the town. He campaigned forcefully against slavery. He founded Washington University at St. Louis, and has left a number of religious writings, which look forward to Eliot's own, although he did not follow the Unitarian creed. Walter Eliot was, for example, interested in the nature and meaning of martyrdom, a theme which later preoccupies his grandson, and he was regarded as 'a conservative force in a liberal church'. Two of Eliot's uncles entered the Church, but his father, Henry Eliot, preferred to go into business. He became successful in the brick trade, which was important in St. Louis, and although he had broken with the family tradition to the extent of not entering the Church, he remained very attached to the family and spent time collecting information about its members. He died in 1919.

Mrs. Eliot came directly from Boston when they married. She rapidly attached herself to the family and followed it in various ways. She engaged in social work, as did her eldest daughter Ada, who wrote three books on sociology between 1920 and 1937. Mrs. Eliot was also an ardent devotee of women's rights, and a writer herself. In her writing can be seen the same interest in technical innovation which is vital to Eliot's writing, although she was not very successful. She wrote a dramatic poem, on the life of Savonarola, which Eliot published in 1926, at a time when his own interests were turning more strongly to drama.

His grandfather and his mother clearly contributed to Eliot's development as a writer, and especially as a religious poet. His father gave him the business-man side which led him to a bank, and later to his highly successful career as a publisher, though it is also true that other American poets of his generation, Frost, Wallace Stevens, William Carlos Williams, have found it necessary to have a job besides that of being a writer, and that this was very much in the tradition of earlier poets, who were most often diplomats or politicians, like Chaucer or Spenser, Milton or Swift. Only in the 19th century did this change.

Eliot was at day-school in St. Louis until 1905, when he went for a year to a boarding school, and then to Harvard. He was highly regarded at school, and in 1900 won a gold medal for Latin. Theodore Dreiser describes the St. Louis of 1892 thus:

Never in my life had I seen such old buildings, all brick and crowded together. . . . Their interiors seemed so dark, so redolent of old-time life. The streets also appeared old-fashioned with their cobblestones, their twists and turns and the very little space that lay between the curbs.

There was also in St. Louis a firm of furniture wholesalers called Prufrock-Littau.

In 1897, Henry Eliot built a house for his family holidays at Eastern Point near Gloucester in New England, where the family had been accustomed to taking holidays for some time. While there, Eliot became a proficient yachtsman, and sailing images are frequent in his work. Eastern Point is near Cape Ann off which are three rocks known as The Dry Salvages. Both places later became titles of poems.

He began writing at school, and showed technical proficiency as early as 1905, and a sense of humour, since his earliest published piece is rightly marked 'Doggerel licence No. 3,271,574'.

At Harvard from 1906–10, Eliot pursued a wide-ranging course of studies in language and literature: the Classics, German, French, and English Literature, and comparative literature. He was introduced here to Dante and to Donne, two poets highly influential on his later writing. He heard lectures from two people whose attitude to tradition was also developed in him, Irving Babbitt and George Santayana. Finally, the Harvard of that time was very enthusiastic about drama, and the prospects of a revival. An article in the *Harvard Advocate* of 1st June, 1908, the magazine which Eliot later helped to edit, announced: 'Of course, we all write plays.' In that year Eliot read Arthur Symons's book *The Symbolist Movement in Literature*, which introduced him to the poetry of Laforgue. This prompted him to his first period of what might be called mature writing. Between 1909 and 1912, Eliot wrote a group of the poems later published in the collection *Prufrock and Other Observations*. During this period also, after graduating in 1910, Eliot spent a year at the Sorbonne University in Paris, where he read many of the important contemporary French writers and their immediate predecessors. This reading developed the seeds sown by Laforgue and largely confirmed Eliot's development in what has been described as the 'Modern Movement'. In the summer of 1911 he was in Bavaria, where he completed *The Love Song of J. Alfred Prufrock*, and where he met Hofmannsthal, one of the most important German writers in the Modern Movement, and a writer also interested in the revival of classical drama.

Eliot returned to Harvard in 1911 and entered the graduate philosophy school, where he pursued a basic course in philosophy but also read Indian and Sanskrit literature and philosophy. He took boxing lessons at this time, regarding it as rather necessary to force himself not to become a withdrawn person, which being shy he was liable to do. His friend, the poet Conrad Aiken, tried in London at this time and later to find publishers for Eliot's poems, but was unsuccessful, and although Eliot was subscribing to *La Nouvelle Revue Française* and thereby keeping up his French interests, he was not writing anything and was set fair to pursue the somewhat dry career of the Harvard philosopher. In 1913, he was President of the Philosophical Club, and in the next year set out for Germany to study at the University of Marburg—the natural development of the Harvard philosophy student. When the First World War began, he went to Oxford, and continued to study his subject at Merton College until 1915. Being short of money, he took a job as a schoolteacher, first at High Wycombe, then at Highgate Junior School, and from there sent off his thesis on the philosopher, F. H. Bradley, in the spring of 1916. This was the last gesture made to the career of professional philosopher; he never returned to Harvard to take his doctor's degree. In 1964, when the thesis was eventually published, he reckoned not really to understand it. There is, at the same time, something accidental about his settling in England and becoming a poet at this time. First the outbreak of war, next in September 1914 an encounter with Ezra Pound in London, and an introduction into the lively literary circles of the London of that time, and finally his marriage to an English girl in July 1915: these things determined the course of his later career.

The meeting with Pound was of the greatest importance. Ezra Pound is one of the most remarkable figures to emerge from this period of literature. His standing as a poet has yet to be determined. His influence as a personality is clear and extraordinary. He was as flamboyant as Eliot was prim, and he was one of the key figures in the second decade of the century in London. He left after that and became almost as important in Paris. He found a publisher for Eliot's poems: first, the American magazine,

Poetry, then various English magazines, finally leading to the publication of the first collection of poems in 1917—*Prufrock and Other Observations*. This contained the group of poems written at Harvard and in France and Germany, together with a less important group of short poems on Boston, written at Oxford in 1915 (the group *Morning at the Window—Hysteria*). These Boston poems are a final reduction of a great deal of much more diffuse satirical writing on Boston which Eliot and his friends went in for as undergraduates.

New poetry was circulated then very much as it is now, in the little magazines. Undergraduate magazines carry much poetry of very mixed quality. Then the young writer finds other magazines, little-known ones perhaps like *New Departures*. Next, his work, provided it is showing some quality, is accepted by magazines of much greater importance and wider circulation such as *Encounter*. Finally, the various poems are collected in a volume by an enterprising publisher, or a press like the Scorpion Press which specially publishes new poetry. This pattern was set in the early years of the century. Eliot's magazines were *Poetry*, *Blast*, *The Little Review*, *The Egoist*, *Dial*, and then in due course his own magazine, *The Criterion*. His first collection was published by *The Egoist*, and the next by The Hogarth Press, the press directed by Leonard and Virginia Woolf, who were part of that exciting literary world which Eliot had entered into.

Pound and his friends lived in the neighbourhood of Kensington. In 1916, Eliot met Clive Bell and through him eventually the writers and artists of another important London region, Bloomsbury. Centred around the Woolfs and the Bells, this group was also linked with E. M. Forster, and, via Middleton Murry, with D. H. Lawrence, whom Pound summed up succinctly: 'detestable person, but needs watching'. The writers associated with Pound were such as Wyndham Lewis, Ford Madox Ford, W. B. Yeats, and in due course, James Joyce, though he was never very much part of these literary coteries. Nevertheless, even from so brief a summary as that, it is easy to see that Eliot now moved among the people who were in due course to be regarded as the most important writers of the period.

All of them possessed a vital, even violent dedication to the arts. They wrote poems, plays, and novels, they painted, they did not write music but delighted in it, and especially in the ballet, which became extremely popular in London during these years. They endeavoured to preserve the very highest standards of creative art, and of what they regarded as the European culture. Despite the coterie appearance, they were not at all parochial, and were in touch with all the latest similar work on the Continent.

In 1917, Eliot gave up teaching, and entered the foreign department of Lloyds Bank, where he worked until 1925. He kept up a vigorous life of writing, and several times became ill with overwork. He was not called up for service in the American Navy during the war, and was engaged at that time on the caustic, wry poems of his second collection published in 1920, though again all the poems had been already published in various forms since 1918. Most were written in 1917, though the most important, *Gerontion*, was written in 1919 and marks the start of what is generally regarded as the darkest and most bitter period of Eliot's career. At the same time, however, he begins during this period to gain some reputation. He is being read at the universities and the more perspicacious tutors are recommending him, though it was probably more often the pupils who brought the poet to their teachers, as in the case of W. H. Auden to Nevill Coghill at Oxford in 1926.

In the autumn of 1921, Eliot wrote a draft of his most famous poem, *The Waste Land*. He gave it to Ezra Pound in Paris, who edited it and made various suggestions, which led eventually to the poem which was published in 1922, in the magazine *The Criterion* which Eliot was editing himself, financed by a patron. It was received with some bewilderment by many readers, and still is. It was also acclaimed by those who already had some feeling for and understanding of the techniques which the poem used, which are as startling now as they were then. Eliot has had many imitators, and he has influenced many who have not imitated him. No poet who has followed him and who has been well received has used quite the techniques which this remarkable poem uses, except Ezra Pound himself, and it will remain a curious point how much the special quality of the poem, which is not quite like the rest of Eliot's work, depends on its handling by Pound. (The manuscript, with Pound's annotations, has recently been acquired by the Berg Collection of the New York Public Library. This important event will lead to new studies of the poem. An account of the MS can be found in *The Times Literary Supplement*, No. 3480, of 7 November, 1968.) In 1925 Eliot joined the new publishing firm of Faber and Gwyer, formerly The Scientific Press, which was already expanding its interests. From this time, Eliot's reputation grew, though it remained necessary for F. R. Leavis in 1932 to draw particular attention to the high quality of his poetry, in a manner which indicates that this was by no means accepted in academic circles.

Eliot edited *The Criterion* from 1922 until 1939, when he closed the periodical himself, visualising the breakdown of communications in Europe during the war, and thence the breakdown of one of the things for which the magazine had most strongly stood, the integrity of European culture. It had never published or reviewed a narrow field of work, but had received contributions from all over Europe.

Never a prolific poet—he thought in fact that a poet should probably write as little as possible—his work in the twenties falters somewhat. Apart from the pieces which eventually became *The Hollow Men*, and the two fragments of the play *Sweeney Agonistes*, he wrote no poetry for publication between 1922 and 1927. In that year, he became a British citizen and was confirmed in the Church of England. The poetry which follows these steps is of a different tone from anything that precedes it, though there is not by any means the division between the two phases of his work that has been sometimes identified. In the same way as qualities in the love poetry of the young libertine, John Donne, are discerned in the intense religious verse of the later Dr. Donne, Dean of St. Paul's, so the same qualities run through Eliot's work in both its phases. He is at all times a religious poet in that he is concerned with the relation between man's worldly experience and his sense of an order beyond him. At times that order is almost invisible through the chaos which obscures it, but its presence is implicit in all Eliot's major poetry.

At the beginning of the second phase, the poetry was, however, certainly more obviously religious, as the titles of the poems suggest: *Journey of the Magi*, *A Song for Simeon*, *Ash Wednesday*, which at once suggest a close association with the Christian religion.* In the same group of writings are *The Rock* and *Murder in the Cathedral*, with very specifically Christian subjects. All these poems reflect the stage of Eliot's thinking and feeling about the religion he has adopted and are a stage in his intentions to communicate that religion. In the thirties he became an authoritative figure and he set out to use that authority to further the Church he had attached himself to. In 1939, he published his *Idea of a Christian Society*, which is the straightforward statement of some of the ideas in the poems and plays. His life was now that of an established literary figure, director of Faber and Faber, editor of an important periodical, lecturer, churchwarden. In 1932, he returned to America for the first time since a brief visit in 1915, to lecture at Harvard and Virginia: the lectures were later published as *The Use of Poetry and the Use of Criticism* and *After Strange Gods*.

At this time Eliot was developing a practical interest in drama. He had always had this interest (witness his mother's dramatic poem, the craze for drama at Harvard, Pound's persuading him to translate the *Agamemnon* of Aeschylus in 1920, the earlier interest in Greek drama from Hofmannsthal, as well as many essays about drama and especially poetic drama, and the fragments of a comic melodrama, *Sweeney Agonistes*, the only considerable work in an otherwise dry period), but it was not until after the change of mood in his writing, and until he began to discover a need to reach a wider audience that he came to look more closely at the problems of writing for the stage, working

---

* There is a certain formality in the mode of publication of this time too. Although the major work, *Ash Wednesday*, is published in the same way as the earlier poems, first in part in periodicals, then in a final version in book form, the minor poems are published annually in a series known as the *Ariel Poems*, published as greeting cards for Christmas, with a suitable painting. Toe poems are for an occasion and are accordingly limited, though two of them, *A Song for Simeon* (Sept 1928) and *Marina* (Sept 1930), are of the highest quality.

with small theatrical groups in London, and associating with E. Martin Browne in the creation of a pageant, *The Rock*, in aid of a church building fund. Then came his first complete play, *Murder in the Cathedral*, produced in 1935. It is sometimes suggested that this marks a return to a fuller creative period after a less vital time. The poems of 1927–31 are for the most part less striking and less memorable than those that precede and follow them. Nevertheless, *Marina* is regarded by some as one of Eliot's finest poems, and *Ash Wednesday*, although remote and perhaps thin in comparison with *The Waste Land* and the *Four Quartets*, has passages of refined and purified delicacy which can become as attractive as the richer verse.

In 1936, the second *Collected Poems* appeared, containing the first Quartet of the *Four Quartets*, *Burnt Norton*, written in 1935. The three later Quartets, *East Coker*, *The Dry Salvages*, and *Little Gidding*, complete this last major work. There were also four plays to follow *Murder in the Cathedral*, all formed of material from contemporary aristocratic society (a penchant for the aristocracy was one of Eliot's foibles). These later works show the same profound exploration of the religious life as the more obviously Christian poems, but now there is an attempt to examine this life, without constant recourse to the traditional symbols and ideas. The four plays were *The Family Reunion* (1939), *The Cocktail Party* (1949), *The Confidential Clerk* (1953) and *The Elder Statesman* (1957). Except for a few slight pieces of verse, these plays completed Eliot's poetic works. He continued to publish essays in various collections up to a final collection (published posthumously in 1965), which he had been preparing before he became ill in 1964. He was awarded the Order of Merit, and the Nobel Prize for Literature in 1948. His first wife died in 1947. He married again in 1957. He died in London on 4th January, 1965.

The most striking impression which memories of him as a person give are of his appearance. Whatever else his friends recall, nearly everyone comments on his dress, his precise, proper, dark jacket and striped trousers, which might almost have been a deliberate disguise. Occasionally there are glimpses of him in a more flamboyant costume, and a hint that there was a touch of the dandy in him, but these are rare. He is recalled as tall, pale, thoughtful, absorbed, speaking in measured and solemn tones even when humorous, and in such a way that you could not really tell whether he was being humorous or not. His humour comprehended the music halls in which he delighted, and English nonsense verse, such as of Lewis Carroll and Edward Lear, to which he added in 1939 the remarkable *Old Possum's Book of Practical Cats*, a set of nonsense rhymes about cats which reveals the poet's brilliance at his craft of verse.

There are anecdotes which reveal a remote and melancholy humour with the potent implications of profundity which made it disarming and slightly weird. William Empson recalls:

> There was a party (I forget everybody else in the room) where Eliot broke into some chatter about a letter being misunderstood. 'Ah, letters,' he said, rather as if they were some rare kind of bird, 'I had to look into the question of letters at one time. I found that the mistake . . . that most people make . . . about letters, is that after writing their letters, carefully, they go out, and look for a pillar-box. I found that it is very much better, after giving one's attention to composing the letter, to . . . pop it into the fire.'

Empson comments: 'This kind of thing was a little unnerving, because one did not know how tragically it ought to be taken; it was clearly not to be regarded as a flippancy'. Another anecdote is recorded by Hugh Kenner:

> After *The Confidential Clerk* was produced, a journalist, teased by implications he couldn't pin down, or perhaps simply assigned a turn of duty at poet-baiting, wanted to know what it meant. It means what it says, said Mr. Eliot patiently. No more? Certainly, no more. But supposing, the journalist pursued, supposing you had meant *something else*, would you not have put some other meaning more plainly? 'No,' Mr. Eliot replied, 'I should have put it just as obscurely.'

In both anecdotes, he speaks what he means, and there is a sense in which neither is humorous. On the other hand, both imply a humorous attitude towards the situation, a humorous detachment from it, and even from himself as part of it.

2

Works

Eliot's work is of four kinds: the poetry, which is of the greatest
importance; the drama, which forms an extension of the poetry,
but which, although interesting in itself, is not regarded as such a
central feature of the literary world; the prose work, which has
consisted both of literary and social criticism; and the journalism.
The previous chapter described briefly Eliot's work as editor of
The Criterion.

POETRY

His poetry can be analysed into four or possibly five creative
periods. There is first of all the group of poems of 1909–12,
and of 1915, written in Boston, in Europe, and during his first
year in England. Then there follow the French poems and
the group known as Quatrain Poems, written between 1916
and 1918. In 1919, Eliot began to write some of the darkest
poetry he ever wrote, *Gerontion*, *The Waste Land*, *The Hollow
Men*, and *Sweeney Agonistes*. After the pause between 1922 and
1927, the fourth period begins with the Christian poems, chiefly
the *Ariel Poems* and *Ash Wednesday*, but extending to *The Rock*
and *Murder in the Cathedral*. Finally, though this period is really
no more than a straightforward growth from the previous one,
there are the religious poems which are not specifically Christian,
the *Four Quartets*, and the last four plays.

Although the poetry is not always easy, the general character
or mood of these periods is not hard to identify. The first period
consists of poems much influenced by Eliot's reading of French
writers, in particular Laforgue. They are sophisticated observations of people, of social behaviour, and of urban landscapes.

The last quality is the most striking and the one that marks Eliot off immediately from most previous writers in English. The poetry is of streets and houses and people, not of woods and fields and flowers.

Some of the poems are straightforwardly satirical of Boston society, which Eliot believed to be stifled by propriety and a general cultural decadence. Others are more whimsical and gently ironical on themes of love, though not at all like any old-fashioned romantic love-poetry. Such lovers as there are in this poetry are generally disillusioned and their love unsuccessful; there is a mixture of sharp critical observation, and sympathetic nostalgia, and a poignancy about most of the pictures which makes them different from traditional satire.

The second group of poems is much harsher. The satire is now almost unrelieved by sympathy or compassion, though the French poems do preserve the earlier ambiguous mood. The Quatrain Poems direct a ferocious irony towards people and institutions. The picture is one of a debilitated and rotten civilisation. People are governed by selfish and self-seeking motives; they and their institutions are corrupt or torpid. Money is dominant. The Church is sleeping.

These poems are cosmopolitan; the characters are not specially British, or American, or of any national origin, though the poetry remains strictly urban. We are introduced too to Eliot's central character of his first phase of writing (1909–25), Sweeney, who typifies the grossness and decay of the society he lives in. He is animal and unfeeling. He is, you might say, unconscious. Eliot was fond of him none the less, and later said: 'I think of him as a man who in younger days was perhaps a professional pugilist, mildly successful; who then grew older and retired to keep a pub.' The second group of poems is especially character-ised by the quatrain form which indicates a change of influence. Ezra Pound was concerned about precision and economy in poetry at this time, and he influenced Eliot towards these more highly compressed and terse poems. There is also some influence from an earlier French writer, Gautier, who wrote in that style.

The third period of writing both deepens the distress felt at the contemplation of western civilisation in its present state, and enlarges the range and scope of the poetry. Until this time it has been narrow in reference, with the possible exception of *The Love Song of J. Alfred Prufrock*; dealing with people and places and only by implication leading on to wider themes. With the three poems of this period, Eliot takes on a kind of poetry which belongs with what we call major or great poetry. It is not necessarily always good, or successful, but it is the sort of poetry which attempts some overall vision of man and society and the universe. It used to be called epic poetry, and perhaps is still best called that, for *The Waste Land* is in many ways a compressed epic. It does for its period what Virgil and Milton did for theirs, though of course its scale is considerably smaller than that of the *Aeneid* or *Paradise Lost*. It attempts to portray the state of the civilisation out of which it grows, combining especially the history of that civilisation, its present condition, and its understanding of life, especially its understanding of God. *The Waste Land* only does this in a very limited way, but it stands nevertheless in that tradition.

The poetry of this time is fragmented in effect, lacking all normal cohesion. We are obliged to work to understand how the poems hang together. Probably this is because the poet is really striving for a solution himself, trying to find some light in what appears to him to be an impenetrable maze. This is what the intellectual and cultural life of western civilisation appeared to have become, with the long-developing but by this time complete breakdown of the standards and attitudes which had formerly presented some order, the upheaval in religious thought prompted first by such as Luther, again by Darwin, the scientific revolution which in Eliot's youth was gaining rapid momentum, and the World War, which although perhaps less violently upsetting to most Americans than it was to most Europeans, especially the British, was nevertheless a sign of the social turmoil. The poems are bleak in tone, and are often regarded as entirely pessimistic. This is not so. Each of them, especially *The Waste Land*, draws at some point to a conclusion which points a way out of the maze. There is not much faith or hope in the way, but it is there; especially in Part V of *The Waste Land* there is a feeling of buoyancy which operates as a redemption from the wry despair suggested elsewhere.

The two last periods are readily characterised. The poetry of the period 1927–34 indicates a searching for a right way to express Eliot's now established Christian faith. In this period he is mainly doing so through traditional material and imagery of Christianity, apart from the striking and beautiful poem *Marina*, which indicates the solution Eliot will eventually reach towards. His faith is not at all a sudden discovery of ideas which convert the doubt and pessimism to a ready optimism. It is rather the confirmation of the earlier hints towards faith which have now been formally attached to that of the Anglican Church. There is the same doubt, and the same striving to avoid illusions, which Eliot has revealed ever since *Prufrock*.

In the *Four Quartets*, the poet brings together many aspects of his work. These poems combine the drab and grim picture of modern society which had been prominent before with an intricate contemplation of the problems of space and time, life and death, the past and future. They interweave thought and feeling in a complex manner, and finally reveal how it is possible to have perceived all the harsh aspects and conditions of life, to have seen how pointless and futile is much human behaviour, and how corrupt, to have seen how deluded are most of the answers found to account for this futility, and yet to look at life with faith and hope.

PLAYS

The plays are concerned with a more narrow range of topics. First, apart from the experimental fragments which make up *Sweeney Agonistes*, Eliot wrote directly Christian drama: his pageant, *The Rock*, written to order, and in collaboration with Mr. E. Martin Browne, and then *Murder in the Cathedral*. This is about the martyrdom of Thomas à Becket. It tries to bring the meaning of martyrdom across to the audience, and to make clear the importance of the spiritual life, and of realising that this world is not necessarily all, nor our chosen and proven ways of life necessarily the right ones. This, however, makes Eliot sound unduly moralistic, which he is not. These matters are permitted to *emerge* from the play; it is not deliberately didactic.

The later plays are about similar topics, but the setting has been moved from the historical and religious to the contemporary and social. They are basically upper-class drawing-room comedies, with a strong melodramatic element, and can be enjoyed as just that. They have in manner a good deal in common with other plays of the time by writers such as Granville-Barker, Somerset Maugham, and Noël Coward. Underlying this are the same themes which were to be found in *Murder in the Cathedral*: the meaning of martyrdom to the modern world, the place in that world of the person specially aware of spiritual or supernatural experience. Also, the plays are concerned to show people being made aware of their responsibility for their actions, or in fact, being simply made aware.

Although the plays are not deliberately didactic, the characters and action have a kind of artificiality which limits the dramatic impact. They seem too often to be created out of a theory, rather than from experience. This, however, may be a reaction created by the English dramatic tradition. English drama has always resisted literature created to rule, in a way for example that French has not. The French classical playwrights of the 17th century, with whom Eliot was closely familiar, created their plays much according to rules which they believed (sometimes mistakenly) to have been used by the Greeks. They were successful. When English dramatists, Ben Jonson, or Milton, or Addison, or Samuel Johnson, tried the same technique they failed badly and it is an indication of his ability, in view of this part of the English dramatic tradition, that Eliot wrote what is perhaps the only successful drama in English in the classical style, *Murder in the Cathedral*. It may also be a sense of distaste for the 'artificial' drama—more obviously artificial than for example Shakespeare —that makes us react unfavourably to Eliot's plays.

PROSE

The prose writings are controversial. Eliot was a critic whose authoritative statements achieved great currency in academic circles, partly because his prose style was as precise and memorable as his poetry. He seemed to crystallise what one had been vaguely thinking. He took a firm position on most writers he criticised and was largely responsible for a change of taste towards the poets of the 17th century, such as Donne and Herbert and Marvell, who had been out of favour ever since they were unfavourably criticised by Johnson. At the same time, he occasionally produced phrases which seemed to contain a special idea, but which were opaque, and which were used somewhat according to taste. His most important prose writings are contained in the following books:

Selected Essays, Third Edition, 1951.
On Poetry and Poets, 1957.
To Criticise the Critic, 1965.
The Use of Poetry and the Use of Criticism, 1933.
The Idea of a Christian Society, 1939.
Notes Towards the Definition of Culture, 1948.

The criticism develops in three phases. After he ceased writing on advanced philosophical topics, he turned to establishing for himself certain critical standpoints. He declared allegiance to the idea of tradition, and to certain groups of writers; the Elizabethan dramatists, especially those who follow Shakespeare, and the writers known as the Metaphysical Poets. In 1929, he wrote on Dante, an author who greatly influenced him.

When, in 1927, he made clear his chosen faith, his prose writings take on a more authoritative tone. He begins to assert fundamental theories, and to attempt also to make clear his belief in the importance of his religion, and its way of working—this was brought to a clear position in 1939 with *The Idea of a Christian Society*. Then later, his critical writing becomes more gentle, he begins to revise some of his earlier opinions, and to enlarge on the way of thinking behind his poetry and plays in important essays like *Poetry and Drama* (1952). His essays are often very illuminating about his work. It can also act as a barrier, because when you see that a poem or play seems to bear out exactly what Eliot has said about it, then this to some extent prevents you from approaching the work from a fresh and innocent viewpoint. A poem is not necessarily a good one because it does what the author has at some time said a poem should do, as we can see plainly in Wordsworth's *Lyrical Ballads*.

Certain essays are outstanding, both in their relevance to Eliot, and in the influence they have had. The earliest of these is *Tradition and the Individual Talent*, published in 1919. In this essay, Eliot begins to develop the idea which controlled his writing both as a creator and as a critic. He developed its relevance to the practice of criticism in another essay, *The Function of Criticism* (1923). Eliot believed that no writer and no critic could in fact work independently of the tradition into which he was born and in which he was educated. The pattern of literature of the past was an established thing which the young writer inherited. But it changed with each work of a new writer:

> No poet, no artist of any art, has his complete meaning alone. His significance, his appreciation is the appreciation of his relation to the dead poets and artists. You cannot value him alone; you must set him, for contrast and comparison among the dead. I mean this as a principle of aesthetic, not merely historical, criticism. The necessity that he shall conform, that he shall cohere, is not onesided; what happens when a new work of art is created is something that happens simultaneously to all the works of art which preceded it. The existing monuments form an ideal order among themselves, which is modified by the introduction of the new (the really new) work of art among them. The existing order is complete before the new work arrives; for order to persist after the supervention of novelty the *whole* existing order must be, if ever so slightly, altered; and so the relations, proportions, values of each work of art towards the whole are re-adjusted; and this is the conformity between old and new. Whoever has approved this idea of order, of the form of European, of English literature will not find it preposterous that the past should be altered by the present as much as the present is directed by the past. And the poet who is aware of this will be aware of great responsibilities and difficulties.

This attitude is characteristic of Eliot's sense of belonging to an order which operates somewhat beyond the scene of action of the individual, and the essay goes on to indicate that the art of poetry demands a continual surrender to something beyond the individual as he is at the moment. The interaction between the tradition and the individual is the dynamic source of creative writing.

The poet himself regarded the best of his criticism to be in 'the essays on poets and poetic dramatists' who had influenced him, and among these are especially the essays on Elizabethan dramatists, on Metaphysical Poets, and on Dante. Besides these, however, there were what he describes as 'a few notorious phrases which have had a truly embarrassing success in the world'. Two of these are now met with beyond the context of Eliot himself.

'Dissociation of sensibility' is a phrase from his essay on *The Metaphysical Poets* (1921). It is associated with the idea of 'felt thought' and has obtained an importance somewhat beyond the intentions of its original context:

> Tennyson and Browning are poets, and they think; but they do not feel their thought as immediately as the odour of a rose. A thought to Donne was an experience; it modified his sensibility. When a poet's mind is perfectly equipped for its work it is constantly amalgamating disparate experience; the ordinary man's experience is chaotic, irregular, fragmentary. The latter falls in love or reads Spinoza, and these two experiences have nothing to do with each other, or with the noise of the typewriter, or the smell of cooking; in the mind of the poet these experiences are always forming new wholes.

That is clear enough; it is also relevant to Eliot himself as a poet (his observations on other poets often are). He went on to raise the idea into a theory which is rather less satisfactory:

> The poets of the 17th century, the successors of the dramatists of the 16th, possessed a mechanism of sensibility which could devour any kind of experience. They are simple, artificial, difficult, or fantastic as their predecessors were. . . . In the 17th century a dissociation of sensibility set in from which we have never recovered. . . .

This general theory is not easy to apply in practice to a number of writers between Donne and the present day, though we do not doubt the observation about Donne's unified sensibility. Eliot himself later in the essay calls the theory 'too brief, perhaps, to carry conviction', but nevertheless it was one of his phrases to enter the vocabulary of critical jargon.

Another of these phrases is even less satisfactory. That is 'objective correlative'. This occurs in an essay on *Hamlet* of 1919. Eliot has been writing of the particular quality of *Hamlet*, which has to do with Shakespeare's failure to make quite clear what is the central theme of the play. As part of the argument, he writes:

> The only way of expressing emotion in the form of art is by finding an 'objective correlative', in other words, a set of objects, a situation, a chain of events which shall be the formula of that particular emotion; such that when the external facts, which must terminate in sensory experience, are given, the emotion is immediately evoked.

To some extent, this too is clear enough, though the purpose of such a definition is not very clear. It is simply adding another idea to the already complicated chain of communication between the artist and his audience. He means that the words on the page (for these are the only objective things involved) must act as a sort of code for rendering the emotion imagined by the artist from his imagination to the readers.

During the thirties, Eliot's essays take on a rather more severe tone, as if he is campaigning, which, to some extent, he is. Apart from such as *The Idea of a Christian Society*, others like *Modern Education and the Classics* (1932), and *Religion and Literature* (1935), have a tone of urgency rather different from the tone of the literary criticism. Then, in the later part of his life, Eliot went on to write some of his most engaging essays. He is much concerned now with examining his own work, especially as dramatist and critic, and the essays are enlivened with personal observations, and characterised by a relaxed and confident tone. Among the most important are *Poetry and Drama* (1951), *The Three Voices of Poetry* (1953), and *The Frontiers of Criticism* (1956).

3

Literary Background

As might be expected from his view of literature, Eliot inherits something from numerous literary backgrounds. When he began writing, he was already steeped in the literature of Greece and Rome, and of medieval and modern Europe. Later he extended his reading to take in the literatures of the East. It may be possible to identify specific influences at certain times: Laforgue for example, Gautier, Donne, Dante, the Greek dramatists; but a detailed study will be able to identify influences throughout his work from an almost unlimited range of earlier writing. Eliot remained attached to a tradition, but largely detached from any special part of it. For this reason the literary background to his work is perhaps less important than it is for some other writers. You might argue that the best way to look into it would be simply to read Dante's *Divina Commedia*. However, the literary context is important if only in that it reveals to some extent why it was chiefly a pair of expatriate Americans in London who sparked off such an influential poetic movement in English writing. To do this it is necessary to know something of the literary background in England, America and France, and most particularly to know something of Symbolism. When it becomes no longer appropriate to describe the movement in the arts of the 20th century as Modern, it is probable that the poetry at least may well attract the name of Symbolist, which remains at present attached to a number of late 19th- and early 20th-century French writers.

ENGLAND

At the end of the 19th century, the situation in England was this. The novel was unquestionably the dominant literary form.

Although Dickens and George Eliot were dead, the form flourished with Hardy, Henry James, and Conrad. In this field, there was a natural development into modern writing through E. M. Forster and D. H. Lawrence, who were both part of the literary London which Eliot came to. James Joyce brought to it the particular quality of experiment which belonged to the Modern Movement.

The field of drama was less healthy, but was not non-existent as it had virtually been throughout the 19th century except for the popular melodrama. At the end of the century, the comedy of manners received a brief and bright expression with Oscar Wilde, and at the same time Ibsen began to influence British writers, especially Shaw, who did not write plays like Ibsen's for the most part, but was concerned to put social problems on the stage, and was involved in the new life which came into the theatre in London in 1904, when Harley Granville-Barker was producing plays at the Court Theatre. Granville-Barker was also a playwright of promise, though it was never really developed.

The plight of poetry was critical in the eyes of many young writers, for example, Rupert Brooke, who, though he never achieved anything to revitalise the tradition, was well aware of the necessity to do so, and accordingly wrote 'shocking' poems. The vein of poetry first cut into by Wordsworth had been worked out. Writers in the Romantic tradition had become increasingly detached from the experience of life, and were using perpetually a worn-out poetical idiom. The only relief from this was an excursion into sensationalism by the Pre-Raphaelites, and later the followers of the doctrine of Art for Art's Sake, and, curiously, the writers of nonsense poetry like Lewis Carroll and Edward Lear. At the beginning of the 20th century, there were a large number of young writers of quality whose work is now recognised as good minor poetry. These were such as John Masefield, with his tales of adventure, and his nautical background, W. H. Davies who had been a tramp, Edward Thomas who wrote beautiful nature poetry, Walter de la Mare whose insight was certainly that at times of a great writer, and several others whose work is now being revalued and seen in a better light, since it was scorned by the people who followed Eliot and Pound, and who regarded the work of their English contemporaries as worthless. These writers are now known as the Georgians. Between 1912 and 1922, much of their work was collected in anthologies by Edward Marsh and was in fact the main poetry of the period, for the other writers were scarcely known outside the London coteries. Among the Georgians were D. H. Lawrence, and also Robert Graves, who has now emerged as a poet of great stature with the reassessment of these early contemporaries of his, and the questioning of the new 'Tradition' of T. S. Eliot. Nevertheless, none of them was able to break away from the stale words, stale verse forms, stale imagery of the enfeebled Romantic tradition. And, which is in fact more important, not one of them showed signs then of coming to terms with the immense upheaval in thinking and in way of life which was affecting Europe at the time. They were and remained the silver writers of an older Golden Age. The new gold was being smelted abroad. Only one writer who had any close connections with any of these groups of late Romantic writers made the transition to the new tradition, though he did it with resounding success. That was W. B. Yeats, who had been closely connected with the group around Oscar Wilde which pursued the Arts in a sensuous fantasy world of *fin-de-siècle*. A much older man than Eliot or Pound, Yeats in due course took up something of what they brought to English poetry, and eventually wrote poetry which may well be the main thread in the development of the English tradition, where Eliot's must always seem a little outside it.

AMERICA

In America, the situation was bleaker still. Only a nation for little over a hundred years, and recently racked by Civil War, America had not in the 19th century found an identity or developed a strong literary tradition. There had been many writers, one or two of whom had been great, Melville for example in the novel, Emily Dickinson in poetry, and Poe, Whitman, Hawthorne, and Emerson who had been great writers without mastering any particular form greatly. There had also been an important tradition of writing established in New England around figures such as Oliver Wendell Holmes. However, New England was rapidly becoming no longer America. From 1880 there was great expansion which removed social prestige from this one small region and with it literary prestige, though the region did not cease to be influential. When Eliot spent his holidays there as a child, and later as a student, there was a feeling that there was nothing more coming from the region, that it was culturally moribund. The sense of torpor was stronger than was actually deserved, as was to be seen later when new writers emerged at home after the pause, but it helped to account for the heavy pilgrimage to Europe, and for the fact that two of the young men of the time did not come back, though it is important to remember that it had always been a part of the education of an American writer to travel in Europe. Americans were conscious of their cultural dependence on the Old World, and some writers, notably Henry James, had preceded Eliot in settling there.

The tradition of American poetry does foretell something in connection with Eliot's writing, however. There had been various types of poetry. Longfellow preserved in America the English tradition set by Tennyson. Whitman broke most violently with it and wrote out of an ardent nationalism towards the great new nation. Poe explored more curious regions of the imagination, and his contribution to the Modern Movement is one of the curiosities of literary history. Emerson, Emily Dickinson, and, near Eliot's time, E. A. Robinson, wrote poetry which has been called the most properly American (though how to define this has been one of the agonised wrestles of all American writers of the early 20th century). The writing is terse and tough and reserved, unemotional, described as cold. Although Eliot has never been very closely related to this older tradition of his own country, a tradition now taken back to the 17th-century American poet, Edward Taylor, the only American Metaphysical, it may be possible to see something of him in that description; and also possible to pick up fragments from Emily Dickinson, and from Robinson, which suggest comparable attitudes, even if nothing closer.

It is the France of this time which really regenerates poetry, and sets fire to the Symbolist movement which had cosmopolitan results. The curiosity mentioned above is that a particular stimulus to this movement came from the American, Poe, whose works attracted the French poet, Baudelaire. He admired in Poe a quality of indefiniteness: 'I know that indefiniteness is an element of the true music of poetry, I mean of the true musical expression, . . . a suggestive indefiniteness of vague and therefore spiritual effect'. These ideas of musical effect and of indefiniteness were taken up in different ways by later French poets such as Verlaine, Rimbaud, and especially Mallarmé, who was the central figure in the theory of Symbolism. By combining together images it is possible for the poet to suggest a special and unique experience, through the suggestive power of the images, rather than through any logical development. The symbols were not then symbols of the conventional kind, as the cross for Christianity or the swastika for Nazism, but symbols of a special emotional experience of the poets. Edmund Wilson makes clear Mallarmé's ideas:

> Every feeling or sensation we have, every moment of consciousness, is different from every other; and it is, in consequence, impossible to render our sensations as we actually experience them through the conventional and universal language of ordinary literature. Each poet has a unique personality; each of his moments has its special tone . . . and it is the poet's task to find, to invent, the special language which will alone be capable of expressing his personality and feelings. Such a language must make use of symbols: what is so special, so fleeting and so vague, cannot be conveyed by direct statement or description, but only by a succession of words, of images, which will serve to suggest it to the reader.

Poetry which attempts to communicate so particularly private a sensation as is implied here is in danger of communicating nothing at all, which is of course the common charge levelled at

CB

33

many modern poets. Much of Dylan Thomas's poetry is symbolist in this way. And from this precise type of symbolism arises the kind of interpretation where we are to discern a logic of feeling, rather than a coherent development of thought, a feeling worked out in sequences felt to be logical.

Now, whereas this is a narrow kind of poetry, it undoubtedly is part of the whole experience of poetry, and the concentration on this particular aspect at this time had powerful fertilising effects. Yeats regarded a poem as a complex relationship of images, rhythms, and sounds, which in conjunction become a symbol for emotional experiences otherwise inexpressible in words. This belief lies behind such poems of his as *Byzantium*. He enlarged on this:

> All sounds, all colours, all forms, either because of their pre-ordained energies or because of long associations, evoke indefinable and yet precise emotions . . . and when sound and colour and form are in musical relation, a beautiful relation to one another, they become as it were one sound, one colour, one form and evoke an emotion that is made out of their distinct evocations and yet is one emotion. The same relation exists between all portions of every work of art, whether it be an epic or a song, and the more perfect it is and the more varied and numerous the elements that have flowed into its perfection, the more powerful will be the emotion, the power, the god it calls among us.

What happens during the years following Mallarmé is that the poets, like Yeats and Eliot, learn to use this power as part of a poetry which is also founded on the traditional modes of communication. Nevertheless, Eliot remains, for most of his work, the poet who is trying to call up a special and unique emotional effect in his reader, who needs to submit to the evocative power of the images as well as to the apparent 'meaning' of the words. Rimbaud and Dylan Thomas used personal and private symbols very often, and their poetry suffers for it to some extent. Yeats and Eliot also use personal symbols, but build them into patterns which become recognisable as one becomes more familiar with the poems; Eliot's gardens and deserts, Yeats's towers and birds appear repeatedly; and both use the symbol of the rose, which as well as having private associations is one that is deeply imbedded in the literary tradition.

This then was the situation when Eliot came to Europe and to London. English poetry was pale both in style and content. American poetry seemed to be defunct. French poetry had found new resources of inspiration in a form known as Symbolism, and described by Arthur Symons, another of the group round Oscar Wilde, with Yeats, in *The Symbolist Movement in Literature*, which introduced Eliot to Laforgue, though Symons's book did not in fact influence him in itself. In London was Ezra Pound, who with young English writers was in process of establishing a school of poets known as the Imagists, who published a number of collections between 1912 and 1917, contemporary with the much more popular and better known Georgians. The Imagists, as their name suggests, were concerned to capture a fleeting emotional experience in an image. Their theorist was T. E. Hulme, whose five short poems are good examples of their style, though it was not in other cases as narrow as this:

> Above the quiet dock in midnight,
> Tangled in the tall mast's corded height,
> Hangs the moon. What seemed so far away
> Is but a child's balloon, forgotten after play.

ABOVE THE DOCK

More important was their intention towards the language of poetry which was made clear in their 1915 anthology. They insisted that poetry should use the language of common speech and employ the exact word—not merely the almost exact. It must create new rhythms, as the expression of new moods. The Imagists insisted on the poet's complete liberty in the choice of subject and the artistic value of the depiction of modern life, but modern life seen as it is and not as the poet had been taught to see it. And they advised concentration as the essence of poetry. The ground of Eliot's poetry was thus laid. He uses 'common speech'. He is generally conversational, sometimes colloquial, only occasionally 'heightened', and even then he does not depart from the common idiom. His work is concentrated. He deals with contemporary life ruthlessly as it is. He depends a great deal on the suggestive power of images in unexpected juxtaposition with each other to create a special emotional effect. The period was concerned in art with the 'irreducibility' of experience: that is, its uniqueness and the impossibility of expressing it in any other terms than those of itself. You could not therefore say what a work of art meant because in so doing you described something else, which was not really the unique thing. This is an extreme development of the symbolist approach, but shows something about it.

After the Imagists, Eliot and Pound, and Yeats a little later, enlarged on all these possibilities and created important poetry again. They also stimulated new poetry all over the world. The American tradition followed Eliot and Pound somewhat more closely than the English: Eliot has remarked that he has more in common with his American contemporaries than with his English. In England, the first generation to be affected most strongly was that of W. H. Auden. He and his friends wrote poetry with a strong preoccupation with contemporary society. This was the aspect of Eliot's work which seemed most important to them. There followed then a reaction to a more emotional, uncontrolled poetry, represented by Dylan Thomas at the extreme, but in a more controlled form by George Barker, in which you can see an assertion of symbolism as a way of writing, without any particular allegiance to Eliot, except as a re-animator of the language. Finally and recently there is a return to the quiet and careful manner of the Georgians, a kind of poetry which is comparatively easy to understand in logical terms, but which, much more than the Georgians, is taking on the problems of contemporary life, and is using the common idiom. This is the simple pattern discerned so far. We are too near the period to be clear that it is the right one.

4

Historical Background

Eliot remained detached from the popular preoccupations of his time. His comments on day-to-day affairs are infrequent. His reactions to the two World Wars are obscured behind *The Waste Land* and the *Four Quartets*. Nevertheless, he was at once regarded as one of the strongest voices of his age. *The Waste Land* was, wrongly, regarded as an expression of the mood of post-war Europe. Where Eliot belongs most to his age is in the history of ideas, of art, and of attitudes, not in political or social history.

THE SCIENTIFIC ATTITUDE

If there is one great intellectual change which has taken place in Eliot's lifetime—1888 to 1965—it is that all our thinking has been invaded by what might be called the scientific attitude. It is not that the scientific approach to human knowledge and experience can now be considered to be fully worked out; some would say that we were only beginning to discover what the problems are. It is, however, true that the scientific attitude is now beginning to force upon us a way of thinking which challenges a great many of our former assumptions in a way quite as shattering as did Christianity and the collapse of Rome, and as did the Renaissance and Reformation. In Eliot's lifetime, scientific understanding had moved out from its position as an academic affair, only engaged in by the initiated, and affecting society at large only spasmodically through inventions and technological developments. It is with such men as Darwin, Einstein, and Freud that the scientific attitude begins to invade all our thinking in religion, philosophy, and the arts.

In Eliot's lifetime, it has become commonplace to think of

communication by language as an infinitely complex affair, involving what is usually referred to as semantics, the study of meaning. We are more than ever aware that we do not always say what we mean or mean what we say, and finally have become aware of the difficulty of communicating anything at all. This is one of the results of the scientific attitude which submits all experience to ruthless factual investigation in an attempt to describe what is there, what is actually happening, and to reduce that happening, if possible, to its most fundamental elements. As a result, we have begun to scrutinise poetry scientifically in an attempt to describe its component parts, to say how it works, in the same way that we describe how a machine works. Also, in the same way as we prefer a complex and beautiful machine, beautiful perhaps because of its complexity, then so do we admire a complex poem more than a simple one which seems now to falsify, to miss things out.

This attitude does not of course apply only to art and literature in the field of language. We have come to think of a human being no longer as a mysterious compound of flesh and spirit, 'born under one law, to another bound', but as a very complex compound of the same elements that the rest of the world is compounded of, in our case particularly of carbon, oxygen, and hydrogen, with a little of several other elements, working according to the same principles as the rest of the physical world, animated by some kind of electrical process which has not yet been fully determined, but may well be one day. Because of this, we can think of analysing scientifically every aspect of that human being. Again during Eliot's lifetime we have come up against, though have by no means come to terms with, the scientific analysis of personality, the scientific investigation of human behaviour, the science of psychology.

Until the end of the 19th century, there were three different ways in which men attempted to reach an understanding of the side of their nature which is now the province of psychology. These were philosophy, theology, and art, especially literature, because painting and music were more specifically aesthetic activities concerned with the search for and creation of beauty.

The philosopher attempted to explain the nature of things. He was, of course, a scientist, and approached experience in the same ruthlessly logical way as the scientist does today. He was, however, very much less influential in a general way than the scientist is today, though this was probably chiefly for socio-logical reasons: education and technology. The theologian was quite unscientific in that he based his position on what was revealed from a divine source; that in itself was justification enough. He explained human nature, and his explanation was very influential indeed. His 'psychology' became the common one, his explanation of man was generally accepted. The literary artist worked in a much more limited field most of the time, though there are a few exceptions, like Dante. The poet, drama-tist, or novelist was concerned with the individual's psychology, the detailed understanding of the personality, and it was he who was really the forerunner of the 20th-century psychoanalyst, though his purpose was to create a work of art rather than to provide a psychological casebook. Nevertheless, this is what the great writer often did, and it is the trueness of this casebook that to some extent conditions our opinion of his work today. Literature has not been replaced by psychology, but the scientific attitude has tended to turn those who might in another time have solved their puzzles about human nature by writing books in which people acted out their characters, or poems in which the poet himself resolved the conflicts of his personality, to investi-gating the mind on a scientific basis.

A third important influence of the scientific attitude on liter-ature and the arts has been the gigantic advance in technology which has removed from the arts the function which was in the past all-important to them (with the exception of music), of providing an image of life which did not fade. The photographer has taken over not only from the portrait painter but also from the landscape artist, the painter of still lifes, and, when you take the film-maker into account also, the painter of great historic occasions. Everything that happens now is easily recorded on film, or television, or radio, and as well as affecting the art of painting, these three have seriously affected literature in that the

39

detailed record of everyday events has filled the time and interest that in earlier days might have been given to the players and playwrights or to the novelist. The problem here is that during a long period of transition there must be an uneasy relationship between these media and the highest standards of art. It is possible to speak of the art of broadcasting, the art of the cinema, even the art of television, but they are all hybrids: literature, painting, and music simultaneously wedded to a technological device; and they have yet to find their standards.

A new attitude to communication, especially by language, a new attitude to personality, and a new way of presenting and recording what has actually happened: these three have all changed our way of thinking about the arts. In Eliot's lifetime, art has become a specialised activity. Artists have sought for what is most fundamental to the aesthetic properties of their special media. Painting is either a matter of lines, shapes, colours, forms, and dimensions, because these are the basic qualities of what any painting achieves, the scientific bases of any aesthetic effect in painting; or it is an attempt to record the allegedly profound experiences of the sub-conscious which the psychologists have uncovered in our everyday thinking. In both cases, whether the painting is abstract or surrealist, it does not communicate easily with any audience, informed or not. It is *difficult*, for the specialist as well as the layman. The same is true of literature. Writers like James Joyce have begun to explore both the fundamental particles of literature, that is, words, and the way in which they present themselves to the mind both of writer and reader; they have also explored the deeper recesses of the mind. The personality as revealed by the psychologist has provided a considerable impetus to writers, but without coming to it as older writers did by means of imaginative insight into human behaviour in normal if intensified circumstances. Experimental psychology based on the study of normal behaviour has only recently begun to assert itself, but it may now indicate a movement away from the melodramatic patterns of the early clinical psychologists whose conclusions were reached after studying a comparatively small number of probably sick persons.

These ideas may seem remote from the poet who is the subject of this book. He belongs, however, with those artists who have been searching for what may be called the fundamental particles of their art. His poetry, like other art forms, is difficult, not only for the layman but also for the specialist. He has also been part of a body of thinking which has been looking into the myths which underlie our civilisation, and the way in which they may influence us now, or at least the stage in the myth that we may have reached—all of which has resulted from the development of psychology and the attempts being made to reinterpret religious activity according to psychological theory.

In the table which follows, you will find some of the most important events in the development of knowledge which have taken place in the last hundred years, and which have specially influenced the new attitudes described. Very few of them stand alone. For example, where there is a reference to Freud, the other clinical psychologists of his period should not be forgotten (e.g. Kraepelin and Janet). I have included only names and events which will be comparatively well-known.

1859 Darwin's *Origin of Species*.
1866 Mendel's theory of heredity.
1870 First Education Act extends primary education to all.
     Motion pictures developed.
1881 Growth of popular press: *Evening News* started.
1884 Long-distance telephone in use in America.
1885 Pasteur develops inoculation.
     Hertz, and later Marconi, develop wireless telegraphy, leading to radio.
     Daimler develops the internal combustion engine.
1888 First roll film.
1890–1915 Frazer: *The Golden Bough*.
1895 Development of X-rays.
1896 *Daily Mail* begins: price $\frac{1}{2}d$.
1898 Rutherford begins experiments on atomic structure.
1900 Freud: *The Interpretation of Dreams*.
1901 Planck: The Quantum Theory.

1903 Wright brothers fly.

First movies: *The Great Train Robbery*.

Model T. Ford, and first bicycles.

1905 Einstein: First Principle of Relativity.

Colour photography.

1906–10 Picasso and Braque develop Cubism.

1908 Schönberg's first experimental music.

1909 Blériot flies the Channel.

Eliot's first poems.

1910 Kandinsky's first abstracts.

1910–13 Stravinsky's experimental music: *The Firebird, The Rite of Spring*.

1914 First colour film.

1916 Jung: *The Psychology of the Unconscious*.

1919 Alcock and Brown fly the Atlantic.

1921 Wittgenstein: *Tractatus Logico-philosophicus*.

1925 Television demonstrated.

1926 First talking film.

Most of these details represent the first instance of a technological development, a new train of thought, or a new form or technique in the creative arts.

POLITICAL AND SOCIAL BACKGROUND

There are far fewer points at which a knowledge of what political and social developments were going on in the world is important to an understanding of Eliot's work. He is an intellectual poet, and writes as intently as he can about the experiences of the mind of man, and this is true even in the earlier verse when we are aware of a social context for the poems. He is not, however, writing very much *about* that social context, and an interpretation of *The Waste Land* which restricts it to being an expression of the post-war malaise which followed the First World War, is a falsification of its universal significance.

England

The period in England was dominated by two world wars and the rise of the Labour movement, though none of these stimulated Eliot directly to any major writing, and the more one learns about the period the more he seems to be detached from it. His claim in the 'twenties to Royalist and Anglo-Catholic sympathies indicates something of this detachment. It is also worth noting that despite the alleged differences between the time before the First World War and the time after it, Eliot lived his life in a period substantially like that of the present day, a period of rapid communications, of advanced medicine and technology, of the huge popular press, of the popular entertainment industry, of a vast civil service organisation, of the Welfare State, which although brought on by the Labour movement, was by no means the prerogative of the Labour party in its creation, of industrial unrest and economic difficulties, and of the disestablishment of the British Empire. All these were features of daily life in varying degrees from before 1888, though perhaps somewhat less commonplace. Eliot was born into what we should call the modern world, which is one reason why, although some of his most strikingly original 'modern' poetry was written before 1922, approaching fifty years ago, it still deserves the description 'modern'.

America

The history of 19th- and early 20th-century America is very different from that of England. The United States was a new nation whose character and place in the world was still uncertain; and it was a nation split by the Civil War (1861-5) which certainly warded off the kind of illusions which made Britain so surprised and so deeply affected by the First World War. After the Civil War, America was engaged in territorial and industrial expansion. During the period from 1850, when California joined the Union, until 1912, when Arizona joined, America was concerned with establishing the states west of the Mississippi. Thirty states before 1850 were joined by eighteen more before 1912, and there were also the developments in Alaska and Hawaii. There were possible territorial developments in the West Indies and the Philippines in connection with the war with Spain in 1898. There was also a growing engagement in world affairs which operated

43

along with the strong contradictory feeling for an isolated position in the world. The first mood led in due course to the participation of America in the First World War in 1917, and the second to the withdrawal from world affairs which followed it.

In industrial and commercial affairs, there was one issue of some importance in its influence on Eliot. In 1902 and the years which followed, there was a movement in America to expose the commercial racketeering which had grown up most strongly in the new industrial nation. One of the earliest exposures by journalists, who in 1906 earned the title of the 'muck-rakers' from Theodore Roosevelt, was an article by Lincoln Steffens in *McClure's Magazine* in 1902. This article became in 1904 the first chapter of his book *The Shame of the Cities*. It was based on an exposure of business corruption in St. Louis, which had involved embezzlement of municipal funds, protection rackets, and rigged elections. The Eliots were involved on the side of those who wished to bring about the exposure, which led to further articles about the same subject elsewhere. This must have influenced the teenage Eliot towards his embittered projection of the business world, and indeed laid the ground for his view of 20th-century society as corrupt and decayed.

5

Poetic Form

Eliot's poetry challenges us to define what poetry is. What happens to us when we read poetry is not easily described, but before attempting to analyse the more inaccessible reactions and responses that we have towards Eliot's poetry, we can clarify some obvious characteristics which are raised whenever the question 'what is poetry' is asked.

An immediate and rather superficial response is that which declares that poetry is different from prose because it has rhymes and is in verses, or because it has a special kind of rhythm. This is true, but not the whole truth. Verses, rhymes, and regular rhythms are the bones of almost all that is called poetry, though to call a thing poetic does not necessarily mean that it has either verses, or rhyme, or rhythm. If you think of a poem as a body composed of a skeleton, covered with flesh, activated by a nervous system which gives rise not only to actions but also to thoughts and feelings, you have a reasonable image to break down the parts of the poem, without ever neglecting the fact that the poem, like the body, is only 'alive' when all the parts are operating together. The form of a poem is like the skeleton, the words are the sinews, the suggestive power of the imagery the nervous system.

In simple terms, there are two kinds of poetic form, organic and inorganic. The inorganic form is that of verse, rhyme, and rhythm, termed inorganic because it is on the whole constant; it gives an absolute structure to the poem which everyone can see. The organic form is that where there is no rigid and obvious form, where there may be rhymes, rhythms, and even verses, but where these are not seen to be in any controlled or regular pattern, though they do appear to give some kind of shape to the poem so that each time we read it they impress themselves more firmly on the memory and are eventually recognised as the constituents of the form of the poem. Sometimes this is no more than the order of words and when we reach that stage it becomes clear that form and meaning are becoming intermingled in such a way that it becomes meaningless to try and distinguish them.

The inorganic form, such as, for instance, the sonnet, is usually one that can be used over and over again in different poems; the organic form is in each case unique. At this point, it may be valuable to turn to the art of music for an analogy, as we shall have to do several times again, and as Eliot himself has done in the *Four Quartets*. In music there are various kinds of form. There is the sonata form which is constant (though allowing of slight variations), and can be used in any number of different works. This form gives a characteristic quality to much 18th-century music like Haydn's symphonies. There is on the other hand that kind of form in a work of music which is purely based on harmonic relationships within the music itself, such as tone-poems like Strauss's *Don Juan*. Here then in another art we have an example of the distinction made between inorganic and organic form. (It must be remembered that these terms are not being used in the scientific sense, except perhaps with something vaguely drawn from the implications of the static nature of inorganic substances and the growing or vital nature of organic substances.)

REGULAR VERSE FORMS

Eliot, despite his reputation as an experimenter, had command of a great variety of conventional inorganic verse forms. Perhaps this is most obvious in his book of comic verse, *Old Possum's Book of Practical Cats*, where many of the poems are made chiefly attractive by the effects of their versification, notably *Skimbleshanks, The Railway Cat*. However, this facility is quite as obvious in the *Collected Poems*, and especially in the collection which contains some of the most difficult of all the poems from the point of view of meaning, *Poems 1920*. Six of the twelve poems in this group are written in quatrains, that is, stanzas of four lines each, in which the second and fourth lines rhyme. Each of these six is comparatively short. In the past, this form has been used in two ways: as a means of expressing lyrical sentiments in connection with some event or narrative, as in the medieval ballads, or in the ballads of the early 19th century; and as a form for the expression of love, as in Elizabethan love poetry. It has also been used in the service of satire, especially in the 17th century, which is the period of past literature and thought that has most influenced Eliot. John Donne used this form to express intricate notions on the subject of love, often sardonically, and it appears again later in the service of more straightforward satirical ideas. It is a form which imposes conciseness and precision of word and thought, and it is exactly for this purpose that Eliot uses it. You cannot be long-winded in it, for it will become tedious; it is not easy to concentrate on the *Ancient Mariner* for the whole of its length without being dulled by the rhythm in spite of the variations on the stanza, and that poem is only saved by its extraordinarily vivid imaginative effects. Many of the ballads and all the lyric poems that use this or closely related forms are distillations of feeling, so that there is very little unnecessary material. One of Eliot's poems which is connected with Donne is *Whispers of Immortality*. This is a poem of considerable compression which makes vigorous use of the chosen form, as well as other techniques, such as alliteration, which in itself is capable of concentrating and stressing certain effects. The first two stanzas which contain very striking ideas in themselves are made more dramatic by the vigorous terse presentation.

Webster was much possessed by death
And saw the skull beneath the skin;
And breastless creatures under ground
Leaned backward with a lipless grin.

Daffodil bulbs instead of balls
Stared from the sockets of the eyes!
He knew that thought clings round dead limbs
Tightening its lusts and luxuries.

47

The pairs 'skull—skin', 'ground—grin', 'bulbs—balls' exaggerate and make more macabre the horrific portrait of death that Eliot wishes to create. And yet, there is something else that is brought about by the form of the poem. This form with its terseness and dramatic attack is not suited to the expression of grand or tragic emotions. It is too abrupt and matter-of-fact, and Eliot brings to it an ironic tone which diminishes the horror and converts it into a rather eerie shiver. The poet is detached and grimly humorous, and chooses a verse form to reflect his mood. The irony is implied very clearly in the title, which has behind it Wordsworth's *Ode on the* INTIMATIONS *of Immortality*, in which the intimations Wordsworth discerns are quite positive indications of another and persisting condition of life beyond, or at least different from this. Eliot can only hear whispers, and at the end we are not very sure that these are not empty and meaningless whispers.

PROSE POETRY

This form is at the other extreme from the tight quatrains of *Poems 1920*. In one poem, *Hysteria*, and then much more seriously in a translation of a French poem, Eliot writes without any verse structure at all. The writing becomes poetry only as a result of what it says, hardly at all from the way it is said. *Hysteria* catches a moment of experience of special intensity, captured by the descriptive details and the ironical tone. It is similar in effect to the Imagist poems written at the same time by others in Eliot's circle.

The translation is that of *Anabase* by St.-John Perse, a French writer whose work Eliot first read during his stay in France in 1910, and who is strongly linked with the Symbolists. It was made in 1931. Eliot wrote in the prologue to the work, which is in prose both in translation and in the original:

> I refer to this poem as a poem. It would be convenient if poetry were always verse—either accented, alliterative, or quantitative; but that is not true. Poetry may occur, within a definite limit on one side, at any point along a line of which the formal limits are verse and prose. Without offering any general theory about 'poetry',

'verse', and 'prose', I may suggest that a writer, by using, as does Mr. Perse, certain exclusive poetic methods, is sometimes able to write poetry in what is called prose. Another writer can, by reversing the process, write great prose in verse. There are two very simple but insuperable difficulties in any definition of prose and poetry. One is that we have three terms where we need four: we have verse and poetry on the one side, and only prose on the other. The other difficulty follows from the first: that the words imply a valuation in one context which they do not in another. 'Poetry' introduces a distinction between good verse and bad verse; but we have no one word to separate bad prose from good prose. . . .

But *Anabase* is poetry. Its sequences, its logic of imagery, are those of poetry and not of prose; and in consequence . . . the system of stresses and pauses, which is partly exhibited by the punctuation and spacing, is that of poetry and not of prose.

This passage illuminates Eliot's view of form in writing, and shows his allegiance to the attitude which looks for a 'logic of imagery' rather than any more obvious formal or logical structure. *Hysteria*, although slight, has the same qualities; the sequences and the pattern of imagery are those of poetry. It has the basic formal problem in Eliot's poetry, which is sometimes thought to be too 'prosaic'. *Hysteria* and *Anabasis* show quite clearly that 'prosaic' is not necessarily a very meaningful word in this context.

ORGANIC FORM

The other works of the poet, the majority, are not cast in any fully traditional form, and yet are not merely in prose form. The characteristics of their form can be approached by studying the method of composition of one of the shorter poems, *The Hollow Men*, published in its final version in 1925. This method of composition may seem strange and arbitrary to some, but it is indicative of the attitude to form in poetry with which we are dealing. Writers in Greece and Rome wrote according to certain preconceived forms. Accordingly, writers in western Europe in the 16th and 17th centuries, who followed the classical tradition, did the same. Their forms were the ode, the sonnet, the epic, the comedy, the romance and so forth. Each of these had certain characteristics to which the writers conformed, alike in subject, style, and presentation. During the 18th century, something of a revolution took place in men's attitudes to these things, and although certain traditional forms persisted into the 19th century, they were subject to change and modification, and new ones appeared alongside them. Browning, for example, was a considerable formal innovator, employing the dramatic monologue with a complexity that it had never had in its rare uses before, and creating the somewhat remarkable structure of *The Ring and the Book*, which is a complex of monologues wherein a number of persons each examine and analyse a series of events from their particular varying standpoints. Whitman at the same time employed extensively a kind of poetic prose, as Blake, who was perhaps the earliest representative of the new attitude, had done before him. It now became the poet's task to devise a form for his work that most fully expressed the intricacies and particularities of what he had to say. And as each poet was a separate individual, so formal consistency between poets became increasingly rare, though the ode and the sonnet, especially the latter, survived the new attitude. Poetry was to some extent a matter over which the poet had no very firm control, so that some of it might come together by accident, and this is almost how *The Hollow Men* grew.

'THE HOLLOW MEN'

The poem began as remaining fragments of the first draft of *The Waste Land*. It was then published in different combinations of its five parts between November 1924 and November 1925. The sequence of re-alignments and adjustments shows clearly how Eliot regarded the form of a poem. Each group is a final version at its point of publication; at the same time, each is capable of growing into another group or another poem. The chronological sequence was as follows:

November 1924:
    in *Commerce*   'We are the hollow men'
    in *The Chapbook*   'Doris's Dream Songs'

	'Eyes that last I saw in tears'
	'The wind sprang up at four o'clock'
	'This is the dead land'
January 1925: in *Criterion*	'Eyes I dare not meet in dreams' 'Eyes that last I saw in tears' 'The eyes are not here'
March 1925: in *Dial*	*The Hollow Men* 'We are the hollow men' 'Eyes I dare not meet in dreams' 'The eyes are not here'
November 1925: in *Collected Poems 1925*	*The Hollow Men* 'We are the hollow men' 'Eyes I dare not meet in dreams' 'This is the dead land' 'The eyes are not here' 'Here we go round the prickly pear'

The two sections not finally incorporated in *The Hollow Men* in *Collected Poems 1925*, were not apparently published again until their inclusion as Minor Poems in *Collected Poems 1909–35*. There has been no change in the form or detail of the poem since then.

Eliot writes of the poetic mind as 'constantly amalgamating disparate experience . . . in the mind of the poet these experiences are always forming new wholes'. The growth of *Ash Wednesday* also illustrates this very well. *Ash Wednesday* was first published in part, and not in the order it finally achieved. It began to appear in December 1927 (Part II), then in spring 1928 (Part I), in autumn 1929 (Part III), and the six parts came together as *Ash Wednesday* in March 1930, a less complicated growth than that of *The Hollow Men*, but revealing a consistent attitude to the way a poem grows into a final shape.

The Hollow Men at present consists of five sections which meditate on the subject of human nature in this world, and on the relationship of this world to another, the world of death, or eternity. The type of person we are concerned with is very probably that which peoples all of Eliot's early poetry, the figure lost in the confused society, or defeated by it. One of the early versions of the poem was called *Doris's Dream Songs*, and Doris is one of the characters who appears in *Sweeney Erect* and *Sweeney Agonistes*. Doris is one of the rootless, pointless people whom Eliot castigates in his early poems; she is one of those in *The Waste Land* who drift through life without ever coming to any decision, or taking any positive action to make themselves signify as people; they are people who might just as well not be there. Her three songs are personal, and she says that she cannot face the confrontation with death when she will meet the eyes of those in eternity who have faced life squarely, and taken the responsibility of being human beings. She will not be able to look them in the face.

This continues in the later version, but Eliot has ceased to frame it within a single character, whose background we know something of already, and whom, if we wish, we can dismiss as being not like us. The Hollow Men who speak at the beginning might be anybody; the Waste Land is here and now. We, the readers, are the men who are hollow, like Guy Fawkes effigies, or scarecrows. The images of the first section convey economically the necessary aridity and pointlessness: broken glass in a dry cellar means that the cellar has lost its purpose, and so has shape without form and shade without colour, and so on. Everything positive and valuable is negated. And it is the negativeness that is very important. People who have died and gone on to eternity, death's other kingdom, if they look back at all (and the implication is that we ought to be surprised if we discovered they cared), think only of how negative and meaningless we are. They do not think 'what a waste', for we are not 'lost violent souls' who made an effort but in the wrong direction; they think 'how useless'. Eliot's absorption in the work of Dante is important here if we are to understand the pattern of ideas. We are dealing with a similar relationship to that which Dante describes in the *Divine Comedy*. There, there are various types of soul after death; those who have gone to Paradise, those who will go, but have first to remain in Purgatory until they have purged away that which dragged them down, those who have gone directly to Hell, and those who by virtue of their pointless drifting through life have gone to a sort of nowhere, a nothingness which reflects their own vacuity, a Limbo at the outskirts of Hell, where they are as it were excluded from the great scheme of Divine Providence. They are almost worse off than those who, because they denied God, are permanently confined in Hell. In *The Hollow Men*, the speakers are the nothing men; they cannot face the eyes of those who have crossed into Paradise, having chosen Good, and they are not thought of as 'lost violent souls' who have chosen Evil, but at least have chosen.

Section II involves, in a more personal situation, one of the Hollow Men, the poet perhaps, who states that he cannot face the eyes of those in Paradise, which he sees in his dreams (the idea of dreams is used to represent the way in which we might understand the condition of eternity). In dreams we see these eyes only in a deflected and fragmented way, as images of great but poignant beauty. In this section, too, we feel some sympathy for the speaker, which we did not feel when the Hollow Men spoke collectively. We feel for him that he cannot face the eyes of the purer and braver souls, and when he asks for 'deliberate disguises', and asks to behave 'as the wind behaves'—as do the souls in Dante's Limbo, blown hither and thither willy-nilly by the forces which surround them. Why should he take on the harsh responsibility of life, why should he not be hollow? The land in which the Hollow Men live is a dead land, a version of the waste land, a desert in which the gods are of stone and return nothing to those who pray. Still sympathetic to the speaker, we feel for him as he confronts the beauty of those who have achieved Paradise in something as approachable as a fading star. That is the nearest he can get, though he is not without the genuine desire, and sometimes when he wakes out of the dream kingdom, he feels this desire most strongly; but it is thwarted because the only idols he has are stone, lifeless, unrewarding. This leads to the fourth part in which the speaker touches despair; the place is as hollow as the men, there are only the fading stars, lost kingdoms, men grope about no longer able even to face speech which gets them nowhere; all the images focus the potential despair, which is only redeemed after this near approach with the faint hope of 'unless'. He does not quite dismiss the possibility that the star will reappear, the star which signifies the eyes of the blessed, and which also is the many-petalled rose, the symbol of the complex unity of Paradise for Dante. But even this is: 'The hope only / Of empty men'. There is a clear ambiguity here in the placing of 'only', a word for whose placing there are no adequate rules. This phrase means both that the rose is only the hope, and nothing more, of empty men, and that it is the hope of empty men only, not of those who know and act better; and it implies as well that it is the only hope of empty men. Thus it operates both ways, pessimistic and optimistic; this ambiguity is surely deliberate.

Section V is of a different kind. It is a sort of incantatory conclusion, as it were a ritual to conclude the lament, which in itself partakes in some way of the nature of prayer: a confession of the condition of the Hollow Men, with their faintest of hopes. At best they can only say with Gerontion, who features in another poem of this bleak period, 'Think at last / We have not reached conclusion'. Section V expresses what comes between them and the eyes of death's other kingdom. It is the Shadow, a force with no other name than this which, for the Hollow Men, keeps for ever separate every potential from every achieved thing: everything that might have been, never is, because the Shadow falls in between. And it is the Shadow that we see falling on the frag-ments at the end, the fragments of prayer, and of despair, both of which are cut off because nothing, whether good or bad or neither, ever achieves fulfilment for these people. As with *Gerontion*, this poem offers very scanty hope, and demands that the reader faces the human condition squarely, understands the bleaker side of it, but yet preserves some hope and endurance. *Gerontion* and *The Hollow Men* represent Eliot's most grim view of life and form an important part of the whole pattern presented in the *Collected Poems*. As *The Hollow Men* and *Ash Wednesday* represent a whole, created of originally separate parts, so the poetic works of Eliot form another kind of whole, more loosely formed, but nevertheless largely coherent.

In this section, I have attempted to outline *The Hollow Men* in such a way as to show that it does possess some formal unity. The complete exercise demands a similar consideration of the earlier versions and arrangements, in an attempt to discover whether they have such a formal unity of their own, and whether therefore there is genuinely a form of poetry which we can properly call organic. In this analysis of the growth of the poem, we see how the poet has been content to let chance influence the final form of his work. A poem can be both complete in itself, and at the same time a part, or a potential part, of another poem; to some extent all the poems a man writes are part of a continuous creation which is an expression of that man. *The Hollow Men*, with its series of movements, is formally similar to Eliot's three major works in verse, *The Waste Land*, *Ash Wednesday*, and the *Four Quartets*. Each of these consists of a sequence of separate poems linked imaginatively, but not linked in any very obvious pattern of sense or logic. Each one is more articulate than the one before, its formal organisation is more controlled, less apparently dependent on chance factors.

THE DRAMATIC MONOLOGUE

There are three reasons for indentifying the dramatic monologue as a distinct form. It may be a means of dramatising and vitalising an idea, it may allow a poet to give insight into a character which otherwise the reader will only know through the poet's description of that character, and it may provide the poet with a means to externalise some aspect of himself, so that he can build up an overall complex picture out of simpler segments. Eliot has created two important characters into whose mouths he places dramatic monologues. One, the simpler because he is more detached from the poet, is Gerontion, the old man in the first poem in *Poems 1920*. The other is Prufrock. Gerontion represents an attitude to things. He is a tenant in a house, this world, which is not his real home, and he is waiting for rain, the rain of the Holy Spirit, which will relieve his own parched spirits distant from God, the rain which will generate life in his dry dead mind, or spirit. Gerontion is old and desiccated. He has never experienced heroic action which might have given life meaning, he has only dwelt in a decayed house, subject to the sordid domination of the landlord, a cosmopolitan inheritor of mixed and confused cultures, waiting for a sign to show that there is something to wait for; and even when the sign, which was Christ, came, it was of no avail among human beings separated each from each by their alien cultures and their individual oddities. He is aware only that life is a welter of confusions, deceptions, contradictions, in which men long for what they have had and lost without realising they ever had it, and waste or spurn what they have because they do not recognise its worth. As the poem proceeds, he is aware too that the heroic action he thought of earlier is also useless. But despite his knowledge he does not despair. 'We have not reached conclusion.' The spider does not suspend its operations, even though Gerontion is dead, and his disintegrated atoms, like those of Fresca and Mrs. Cammel, are scattered out into the galaxy. Eliot's early poems are peopled with vague and shadowy figures, looming out of the darkness and receding again. De Bailhache, Fresca, Mrs. Cammel are simply concrete examples of anybody. They mean everybody. They have curious, foreign-sounding, cosmopolitan names to suit their purpose, and they are one of the means whereby Eliot succeeds in making particularly concrete and vigorous effects.

Prufrock is the other of Eliot's characters who utters a monologue, and he is not so easy to come to terms with. Where Gerontion represents a frame of mind and dramatises a way of looking at things, Prufrock is much more intertwined with the poet himself; this is even more true of the narrator of the other poems in *Prufrock and Other Observations*. In the *Love Song*, we are given a view of a character from without and within. We have enough information to imagine his situation as he proceeds through the soft October night to the salon where the sophisticated women, one of whom he loves, or thinks he does, are taking tea and indulging in elegant conversation, with music in the background. We know something of his appearance and dress. And at the same time we are intimately bound up in the agonies and intricacies of his confused meditation about the nature of things, his hopes which he knows to be vain, and his final poignant and pathetic acceptance of his hopelessness. The other poems in the first collection do have much in common with this first poem in mood and attitude and language. It may be that they are all spoken by a Prufrock/Eliot compound, though it doesn't matter very much. What the monologue in this case has given us is this vigorous double vision of a certain character thoroughly interesting for his own sake, and for his particular way of looking at experience.

METRE

Eliot's use of metre is very much his own. In some of his earlier poems he used traditional rhythms: for instance, in *Whispers of Immortality*. However, the majority of his poems are written with a particular kind of flexible rhythm, adapted in every case to what he wants to say, and seldom imposed on the verse as a strict form. Eliot does not, however, write *free verse*. English poetry since the 16th century has been largely dominated by a type of metre known as blank verse, that is, an unrhymed sequence of lines in which each line has five strong beats, and five or more unstressed syllables. Marlowe's plays use this metre extensively in its simple form. In the hands of Shakespeare it became much more flexible. Its advantages are, of course, that it is not subject to what is sometimes called the tyranny of rhyme, and it is a line of sufficient length to take in a wide range of expression. It can be both abrupt and expansive, colloquial and grand. After Shakespeare, it went through various modifications in the hands of Milton, Wordsworth, and Tennyson, and by the middle of the 19th century was felt to have been overworked.

Another form of metre which has been frequently used by English poets is that known as the heroic couplet. Here the verse sequence also consists of lines each with five strong beats, and five or more unstressed syllables, but in this case they are rhymed in pairs. This is the characteristic verse of the satirists, Dryden and Pope, and continued to be employed by Byron, and by

Keats, though he used it in circumstances other than satire where its compact and somewhat pugnacious effect is less suitable—in long narrative romances, for example. In both cases, the poet and the reader are strongly aware of the regular and decisive nature of the rhythm. It is necessary when discussing metre always to remember that one individual's interpretation of the rhythm of a certain line may not be the same as another's. Sometimes you may have to place the stress according to meaning, and it is part of the nature of poetry to possess ambiguities of meaning. Also, it seems that some people are less sensitive to rhythm than others, and regardless of the meaning of the piece, are never sure which are stressed and which are unstressed syllables. The experienced reader will be able to identify these things, but what is more important is that he should be aware of the underlying rhythm of a whole passage, the pulse of the poem, that is, to continue the image derived from the components of the body. Eliot's poetry is possessed of a strong underlying rhythm, as can be soon detected if you try to read any of the poems as if they were part of a prose work, and is made even clearer if you listen to any records of the poet reading his own work. However, in most of the poems the number of stressed syllables in each line varies greatly between two and seven (or, rarely, eight). There is not very much to be gained from a close analysis of the rhythms that Eliot employs except in the contexts of individual poems. In *Prufrock*, for example, there is the terse 'Do I dare'; the repetitive rhythm of 'for decisions and revisions that a minute will reverse', where the rhythm implies what a monotonous activity it is, this business of making up one's mind; the languorous rhythm of:

> The yellow fog that rubs its back upon the window-panes,
> The yellow smoke that rubs its muzzle on the window-panes,

where the lines enact the behaviour of the smog. But even in picking out these small points it is important to note that each of the lines mentioned depends for its effect on its relationship with the lines that precede and follow it. And these are the kind of metrical effects which feature in most of Eliot's poetry. It is only towards the end of his writing that he begins to grow towards a rather more consistent metre. It is hard to call it a regular rhythm, but at least in the *Four Quartets*, and in some other places, it is possible to discern a regular use of a line with four stressed syllables. There may be three in some lines, and five in others and there will be great variety in the handling of unstressed syllables, but there is an underlying form in the four-stress line, as if the poet has settled into a contentment in which to write his final work, or as if he had found and perfected an instrument properly suited to his personal expression.

6

Imagery and Style

If the form of the poem is its skeleton, the words and images which the poet uses are its sinews and its nervous system. The poet's style is chiefly identified in the words and images he chooses, and in the way he puts them together. But style does include other characteristics, such as tone. For instance, Eliot might be said to have an intellectual style. This would mean that the reader felt the poetry to be full of ideas demanding close attention. Or Eliot might be said to have a detached style. In this case the reader might mean that the tone of the work did not invite him to identify himself with the poet, or to sympathise with him, for he is never made aware of the poet's presence as he is in Keats's *Ode to a Nightingale*. Both generalisations would have some relevance, but neither would be very satisfactory.

A closer analysis of a poet's style will be reached through an examination of his imagery and his methods of handling words.

In Eliot's case, his use of imagery is of the greatest importance, since its quality is one of the most striking and memorable features of his work. His poems are filled with images of great clarity, visual clarity that is, or, even more precisely, mentally visual clarity. His images strike the mind's eye, which is a combined receiver of all the senses, and of the feelings and thoughts that they promote. When it 'sees' an object, it sees it more roundly than the eye alone; it recalls the feel of the object, and perhaps its taste and smell; it receives various emotive suggestions and remembers associated thoughts, and the total impression is a very different one from the one when you actually see the object in question, in the same way that the memory of the smell of a hyacinth is different from the sensation of actually smelling the flower, because the memory includes other things besides the actual smell.

There are two groups of images in Eliot's poetry. There are simple images, such as similes and metaphors, including symbols, which are single objects, charged with a special meaning because of their contexts, because of what they are compared with, or because of their historical and acquired connotations. The other kind of image is peculiar to Eliot, and might be called 'pictures'.

PICTURES

Eliot's longer poems are not unlike films, because they place before the reader a series of pictures. He has taken up a technique rather like that of his contemporary painters and film-makers. A modern painting is often fragmented in a curious and unfamiliar way so that at first sight it appears to be no more than a jumble of meaningless shapes among which are pieces reminiscent of familiar objects. A good example of this is Picasso's recent series of variations on Velasquez' painting, *Las Meninas*. A film director, also, may use the technique of abrupt cutting known as 'montage', where a total impression of a scene may be built up by a rapid sequence of shots of detail from any parts of the scene, not necessarily put together as the eye would see them—rather more in the way that the memory might record them and recall them later. This technique is used by Eisenstein in his famous film of the mutiny on the Russian battleship *Potemkin*.

What Eliot's poetry has in common with these techniques of painting and film-making is that he achieves his result by combining a series of pictures or images in such a way as to create a unique impression. It is as if the poetry has become non-representational. We enjoy music by feeling something about the sounds; they excite us, make us happy, or sad; and only later by seeing how the music is put together, how its harmonies are built up. Each piece of music is unique and each piece of music is 'meaningless' in the sense that it does not refer to things outside itself. This is not exactly true of the poems that we are considering; but at the same time, in the sense that the beauty of the thing may lie in the sequence of pictures, real or imaginary, as they pass like the notes and chords in a piece of music, they do have something in common. The poems have some sort of referential meaning to objects and ideas with which we are already familiar, and it is because of this, and because we are looking to understand the poems in the same way perhaps as we understand a story or an argument, in a *logical* way, that we start to flounder and end up by saying that the poem is incomprehensible.

When we read Keats's ode *To Autumn*, we feel sensations akin to those we feel when we actually see an autumn scene and smell its smells and taste its fruit, intensified by the poet's powers of concentrating an amount of detail that we should probably not absorb in any actual situation. We do not stop to respond to this detail logically: we take in the whole effect instinctively.

However, in this case, we feel that the sensation is straight-forward and logically coherent, and are not worried by the fact that the poem has no *meaning* which can be expressed in other words. It is enough to say: 'This poem is about autumn.'

In Eliot's poetry, his pictures work in a similar way. This passage in *The Waste Land* is about the hyacinth girl, and that is all there is to it. We are to respond instinctively to its suggestions. In this case it is possible to demonstrate what is intended:

> 'You gave me hyacinths first a year ago;
> 'They called me the hyacinth girl.'
> —Yet when we came back, late, from the hyacinth garden,
> Yours arms full, and your hair wet, I could not
> Speak, and my eyes failed, I was neither
> Living nor dead, and I knew nothing,
> Looking into the heart of light, the silence.

35–41

This passage would not cause any particular difficulty if part of another sort of poem, a romance let us say, where we are familiar with the two speakers, and know why the hyacinths were so important, and what there was in their relationship to promote the curious experience of suspended animation which the man has. And we are meant to respond, at first at least, to this piece as if it were part of such another poem, for it is clear enough that the two are or have been in love, that this love has been symbolised for the girl by the hyacinth, a flower of strong yet clear sensuous impact both in scent and appearance. The man has suffered some remarkable emotional experience as a result of which he has seen beyond the superficial appearances of things into the 'heart of light'.

The special problems arise from the juxtaposition of passages like this with other passages of apparently completely different import. It is then that we begin to complain that the poem has ceased to communicate anything. In the preface to *Anabasis*, Eliot enlarges on the idea of a 'logic of imagination':

> . . . any obscurity of the poem on first reading, is due to the suppression of 'links of the chain', of explanatory and connecting matter, and not to incoherence, or to the love of cryptogram. The justification of such abbreviation of method is that the sequence of images coincides and concentrates into one intense impression of barbaric civilisation. The reader has to allow the images to fall into his memory successively without questioning the reasonableness of each at the moment; so that, at the end a total effect is produced.
>
> Such selection of a sequence of images and ideas has nothing chaotic about it. There is a logic of the imagination as well as a logic of concepts. People who do not appreciate poetry always find it difficult to distinguish between order and chaos in the arrangement of images; and even those who are capable of appreciating poetry cannot depend on first impressions. I was not convinced of Mr. Perse's imaginative order until I had read the poem five or six times. And if, as I suggest, such an arrangement of imagery requires just as much 'fundamental brainwork' as the arrangement of an argument, it is to be expected that the reader of a poem should take at least as much trouble as a barrister reading an important decision on a complicated case.

This passage helps us to understand the working of the 'pictures' in Eliot's poems. First, a poem that uses only a single picture, *La Figlia che Piange* (The Girl who Weeps), is one of his most enchanting poems, and contains one of the most obvious examples of a collective image. The important experience of the poem is the picture of the girl weeping in the autumn sunshine, at the top of a flight of stone steps near an urn, with her hair falling 'over her arms and her arms full of flowers'. The 'I' in the poem is an older man looking back in his memory at a parting from a girl he has loved. He asks first in the epigraph, 'O maiden, how should I recall you'. He had, we believe, chosen his time to leave this girl, he had brought her flowers, and now much later he thinks back to what he thought might have happened, to her sudden gesture of 'pained surprise', and her flinging the flowers away, which even though painful, would have been a beautiful memory for him. This is how he 'would have had' things happen (the 'him' in the poem is the speaker himself in his youth), and he comments now with a mild bitterness that it would have been like the soul leaving the body which it has made use of and discarded, and he wishes he could find a way to work these partings; and I think we are to believe that other partings have occurred since the special one he is thinking of in this poem. He wishes there was 'Some way incomparably light and deft' whereby two people who have loved each other should, at the proper time, when love has faded—the speaker is a little cynical—know how to part, with 'a smile and a shake of the hand'. The beauty of the picture and its effect of unspoken feeling prevents us from taking this man's cynicism brazenly. It is a cynicism which combines with itself a considerable tenderness. It is that brand of cynicism which goes better by the name of resignation, or if that word implies defeat, then say a willing acquiescence in the nature of things and especially human nature. The picture is not, however, quite the simple one the man looks back on at first; it is not just the what-might-have-been picture. The girl made no gesture of pain; she held the flowers, and simply turned away, and the picture becomes incomparably sad, for her acceptance is not what he wants. She accepts indeed but with suppressed feelings, which at once strike this sensitive man, who, though the action has been irrevocable, has been compelled to live with the memory of the moment. He wonders whether he should not have parted from her, but stayed. Then he would still have had the girl. Now he has a 'gesture and a pose' and is troubled by his unresolved thoughts, for the gesture and the pose are of great beauty, and this man is surely a collector of such experiences; and yet the way the girl reacted to the situation was such as to suggest that she herself was of very much greater value.

Everything in this poem seems to me to depend on the reader's reaction to the picture, perhaps on his power of evoking similar circumstances in his mind's eye. Without a sensation of that 'image', I do not see that it is possible to share in the speaker's experience, or to understand how the delicate balance is achieved between the cynical detachment from all the finer emotions associated with human relationships of this kind, and the deep regard for the validity of such emotions, which is shown in the fact that the girl did not react as the man had expected.

The Waste Land is a sequence of such pictures. I have already mentioned the effect of the passage in Section I describing the episode in the hyacinth garden and its consequences. It seems to be a moment of love which leads to a mystical perception, a perception, if the passage is taken on its own, of considerable value. The man has seen something of great depth even though, because it transfixes him in a sort of life-in-death, he is not apparently able to communicate it. Another picture in this first part of *The Waste Land* is that of Marie in Germany. As with the hyacinth garden, this is a picture of brightness and light, with sparkling water.

In the first picture, there is rain, followed by sunlight; in the second, there is the girl's wet hair, and at the same time the hyacinths giving the colour, and by implication the sparkle (there is already some interaction between these two pictures, coming as they do within twenty lines of each other). Both pictures are of a garden. The picture which Marie recalls is not, however, one which leaves us with a positive effect, as does that of the hyacinth garden. Marie first relates a moment in late spring or early summer in Munich, at the northern end of the Starnbergersee, in which she, and probably a man, walk, and then take coffee; she asserts to him: 'I am not Russian, I come from Lithuania, I am really German'. (The feminine form 'keine' indicates that it is Marie speaking.) Immediately after this, however, Marie's memory flits elsewhere, and she recalls another picture, of her childhood, when she is out in the mountains on a sled with her cousin, this time in winter. In this memory, there is something of value. While sledging, Marie experienced a feeling of freedom, which by implication she has now lost. Finally, completing the complex, yet slight study of this person, in the last line of the first paragraph there is another picture:

I read, much of the night, and go south in the winter.

The lady is restless and bored, and she is also rich enough to 'go south in the winter'. She is aristocratic; moves in cosmopolitan circles; growing old, she has, once at least, had an experience of enduring worth to her, even though it is such a trivial one as a sled-ride, but now her life is reduced to fragments in her memory. There is added to the composite picture a touch of fear. She disclaims Russian origin because she is perhaps in a political situation where she needs to be truly German.

The point about these pictures is that even though they are slight and fragmentary, they lead us because they are so clear and natural to conjecture in this way about the figures that appear in them, to fill out the pictures, and then to try to discover what they stand for in a more general way. The portrait of Marie is presented in three parts, of which the last gives us a large hint of the general meaning of the whole. Marie's is a life of some potential wasted, not so much by any action or intention of hers, but simply wasted by inaction, a failure to grasp experience.

The picture of the hyacinth garden has similar implications. It is brought into close contact with two other pictures, both very brief, which change its general import:

> *Frisch weht der Wind*
> *Der Heimat zu.*
> *Mein Irisch Kind,*
> *Wo weilest du?*
>
> You gave me hyacinths first a year ago;
> . . . .
> Looking into the heart of light, the silence.
> *Oed' und leer das Meer.*

31–5, 41–2

66

The first piece of German means 'The wind blows freshly to the homeland. My Irish child, where do you linger?', and is the song of a sailor in Wagner's *Tristan und Isolde*. The second, from another part of the opera, means 'The sea is desolate and empty'. These passages imply another romance, a well-known one this time, in which the result was tragic. The sailor, feeling the wind blowing towards his homeland, thinks of the girl he loves. This is put next to (or, in the language of film, *cuts* to) the hyacinth garden episode. Then comes another cut to an image of emptiness and desolation, which leads us to believe that the man's vision into 'the heart of light' was also, either at once or later, a similar vision of desolation. After all, 'the silence' need not be a perfect silence, the silence of things at rest; it could be the silence of emptiness, the silence of the void. Space is said to be frighteningly silent; Ingmar Bergman has recently made a film called *The Silence* which studies the failure of communication between people, the silence between people who, although they speak to each other, do not make any kind of contact. Here then, the sharp clarity and realism of the picture, set next to the image of desolation, have a clearly ambiguous effect, not entirely dissimilar from that of *La Figlia che Piange*, where the experience of love strikes two ways. One way is beautiful and moving to such an extent that all one's questioning of life ceases, because one has found satisfaction. The other is bleak and vacant so that all one's questioning of life ceases because one has found an answer, albeit a grim and unrewarding one.

The pictures in *The Waste Land* are numerous. To confirm what I mean by pictures, I will list a few of them. There is Madame Sosostris, the clairvoyante; the crowd crossing London Bridge on a winter morning, another picture of desolation; the two interiors of Part II: the exotic boudoir of the first lady, which we are to visualise closely, and the bar in the pub of the second, of which we only catch the atmosphere; there is the Thames; and Mr. Eugenides; the typist and her sordid clerk; finally, in the last section, the vaguer, mistier pictures of crowds, in anger and revolution, and remote hordes, interspersed with sudden briefer pictures of individuals, now rather supernatural in tone; the mysterious third person who can only be seen as you walk along while you are gazing ahead, and never when you look round to see who it is; and the surrealistic woman playing music on her stretched-out hair as if it were a violin.

This sequence of pictures is central to *The Waste Land* as poetry. Whatever you understand from it will vary according to your interpretation of these pictures and the other images and symbols, and will vary according to your own beliefs about society and love and religion; no one should expect to achieve a definitive interpretation of this poem. What *is* definite is the vitality and realism of these pictures as they pass by like shots in a film, where each shot has been carefully composed to force the audience to observe its sharp outlines and its basic form.

SIMILES AND METAPHORS

Eliot does of course make use of conventional imagery. He uses straightforward similes and metaphors, and he uses them in the usual way, even though some of them may be rather startling. We do not need to search for suitable examples. On the first page of the *Collected Poems*, we find:

> When the evening is spread out against the sky
> Like a patient etherised upon a table;

and:

> Streets that follow like a tedious argument
> Of insidious intent . . .

The streets niggle and persist until eventually they wear down the walker, just as an argument of the kind described would wear down the arguer. The evening is torpid and apparently lifeless like a patient under anaesthetic. These are obvious similes whose import is nothing more than to give a clear impression of what the objects described are like; or, if anything more, to give an impression of what the emotional impact of those objects is.

For metaphors, we have only to move on a few lines to find this:

> The yellow fog that rubs its back upon the window-panes,
> The yellow smoke that rubs its muzzle on the window-panes,

Licked its tongue into the corners of the evening,
Lingered upon the pools that stand in drains,
Let fall upon its back the soot that falls from chimneys,
Slipped by the terrace, made a sudden leap,
And seeing that it was a soft October night,
Curled once about the house, and fell asleep.

The fog which is literally yellow and literally lingers on the pools
is in every other respect made like an animal, a cat most likely. As
in the case of the two similes mentioned above, the image may at
first sight seem startling or unusual, and Eliot does seek out
unusual images. At the same time, he uses these images in a
perfectly straightforward conventional way. It is not hard to
find out what the correspondences are between the object and
the comparison. The fog is made slinkily and secretively and
silently animate, and is thus given a sort of positive power to
cling, even an intention to do so, which, described as simply
inanimate matter, it would not have. In particular, Eliot manages
to convey the way in which fog intrudes into the last little corner,
and also how it operates almost as a solid body collecting the soot
with which the atmosphere is laden.

Continuing through *The Love Song of J. Alfred Prufrock*, we
come upon these:

I have measured out my life with coffee spoons . . .

When I am pinned and wriggling on the wall . . .

To spit out all the butt-ends of my days and ways . . .

   I should have been a pair of ragged claws
Scuttling across the floors of silent seas.

All these are arresting images, demanding that the reader thinks
what the comparison means: life like a series of cups of coffee (or
perhaps literally occupied with nothing but coffee-drinking);
each day passing like a smoked cigarette. The last one is not,
technically, exactly a simile or metaphor, though it operates like
one. Prufrock is like a mindless and primitive creature, a crab;
he goes sideways about things, and gets nowhere even then. He
might just as well be at the bottom of the sea.

Images of this kind are prominent in *The Love Song* but are not very common in the whole poetic works. In later poems it comes progressively more difficult to find simple images. Here is an image from *Portrait of a Lady*:

> The voice returns like the insistent out-of-tune
> Of a broken violin on an August afternoon.

Now the general effect of this image is clear enough. The voice in question is unpleasant to the ear and is furthermore persistent, but this is by no means a simple image. If we are to take 'broken' literally, then the violin would not only be out of tune; it would be impossible to play; and, furthermore, why should this sound be any different on an August afternoon from any other afternoon? The last is easier to answer, for the weather in August may be sultry and oppressive, when the cracked sound would be more grating than usual. But, in fact, this is a simile in process of becoming a picture: some of the pictures are set in a certain time of year, and do not disturb the reader. In the close working of a simile it is hard not to look for something precise, but if we remember Eliot's poetical background of symbolism, we will conclude that this is probably a personal symbol, recalling a certain experience, which *we* can only respond to as it forms part of the emotional effect of the passage of the poem.

Two more images from *Rhapsody on a Windy Night*:

> Every street lamp that I pass
> Beats like a fatalistic drum,
> And through the spaces of the dark
> Midnight shakes the memory
> As a madman shakes a dead geranium.

The first is not so hard. The man is highly sensitive to each lamp as he passes it, and soon the lamps fall into regular rhythm which seems to be telling out his or somebody's fate. The second is more startling, but is most obscure. What the poet sees as he walks along the street one windy night stimulates him to the remembrance of unlikely, confused, and mainly ugly things, as later images indicate. Also perhaps the memories are pointless, they are shaken out of the memory by a force which has no use for them and does not know what it is doing; hence the madman. And they themselves are dead and useless as the flower is that the madman shakes, though they once had vigorous and brilliant life as the particular flower that Eliot chooses, the geranium, had.

An image more like those in *The Love Song* comes a little later in this poem:

> Regard that woman
> Who hesitates toward you in the light of the door
> Which opens on her like a grin.

It is a little nightmarish, this grin, for out of it has come the woman; but also the image means to do no more than convey the nightmarish mood of the scene, with the awful grin in the background which, given a chance, might well develop into diabolic laughter.

SYMBOLS

In Chapter 3, there is a short account of the origins of the Symbolist movement in poetry, and of what effects the poets were striving for when they used symbols. Some symbols used by the French poets were of a peculiarly personal kind, to such an extent that it is not at all easy to discover what the reader is intended to receive from them. The 'suggestive indefiniteness' is pursued to such an extent that any communication becomes a matter of chance. There are such symbols in Eliot's poems, as for example the dead geranium in *Rhapsody on a Windy Night*, mentioned above.

For the most part, however, Eliot's symbols belong more nearly with the conventional symbols, such as the cross for Christianity. They are not always as emblematic as that, but they do acquire a kind of emblematic force in his work. Thus, for example, deserts, dust, and dryness wherever they appear tend to symbolise the desiccation of the spirit, though sometimes they may hint at some kind of purgation. Water, especially as rain, signifies a relief from that desiccation; though, in the form of the sea, it is again likely to mean a purgative, cleansing force. Obviously, in a writer whose work developed over forty years,

71

it will not be possible to identify a constant use of imagery whereby certain images can always be taken to signify or hint at certain ideas. At the same time, there are a few images which obviously took on particular force in Eliot's imagination, of which deserts, dust, and water are prominent. The sea is less so. In *The Love Song*, Prufrock looks to the sea and the mermaids as a way of escape from his drab and pointless life. In *The Waste Land*, the sea purges away all the sinful lusts of the flesh which have corrupted it. In *The Dry Salvages*, the sea represents time, in its aspect of a continuing flow or flux. Fire is either purgative, or pentecostal. It either represents a burning away of corruption and decay, or the arrival of a saving and purifying grace. In other words, it retains its traditional symbolic force, as the destroying fire of Hell, the refining fire of purgatory, or the inspiring fire of the Holy Spirit.

The early poems are full of fog; they are poems also of evening and night, so that we are left with an impression of lost souls wandering in an obscure twilight world.

Finally, there is one group of images, especially in the later poems though they belong to all his work, which clearly have special significance, but which do not have the same kind of tendency to become emblematic as the ones above do. This group centres on gardens, and extends to take in flowers, fountains, yew-trees, birds, and other details associated with gardens. There are prominent instances—*La Figlia che Piange*, *The Waste Land*, *Ash Wednesday*, and especially the *Four Quartets*, where one is specially aware of the importance of this symbol to Eliot, but there are many other less obtrusive references, both to the central image and to its related details, so that the whole group deserves a detailed study beyond the present scope. The gardens tend to be the places where significant things happen, experiences of special meaning to the people concerned, experiences which imply further possibilities of life not yet realised, or perhaps missed. The gardens have the special poignancy of the what-might-have-been. *La Figlia che Piange* contains the strongest garden scene of this kind in the early poems, though there is a garden in *Hysteria* and in *Mr. Apollinax*, while the lady in the *Portrait* twists the stems

T. S. Eliot at the age of sixteen

The village of East Coker in Somerset

'The drained pool' at Burnt Norton in Gloucestershire

Eyes that last I saw in tears
Through division
Here in death's dream kingdom
The golden vision reappears
I see the eyes but not the tears
This is my affliction

This is my affliction
Eyes I shall not see again
Eyes of decision
Eyes I shall not see unless
At the door of death's other kingdom
Where, as in this,
The eyes outlast a little while
A little while outlast the tears
And hold us in derision.

Poem written by T. S. Eliot in his wife's private notebook

The chapel at Little Gidding in Huntingdonshire

of the lilacs in a bowl in her room. The lilacs, as in *The Waste Land*, signify a less sterile, more positive life than she has led, a life she has missed. The hyacinth garden in *The Waste Land* is intensely beautiful, but the experience which takes place there is sterile.

Ash Wednesday has the most haunting garden of all (see p. 75), but there is a new feeling there. The poignancy is not reached through what-might-have-been, but because the beauty of the garden must be turned from and forsaken for the journey among the rocks in the desert. The poem by this means evokes the intense longing of the spirit for the beautiful things of the earth, yet in the face of the necessity to forsake them and move on. Finally, the garden becomes specially the rose-garden in the *Four Quartets*, most prominent in *Burnt Norton*, where it signifies a place of release from the bondage of earth and time, a place of order and beauty, relieved of suffering and futility. The garden in this sense was present in *Ash Wednesday*, though not understood in the same way, and mingled with the garden as a simple and beautiful earthly thing. This garden was also in the early poems though it was not understood at all there, since the spiritual experience which it signifies in the *Four Quartets* was scarcely believed in. It is worth noting finally that Eliot concludes his last play, *The Elder Statesman*, with a garden scene in which the central character achieves peace of mind.

STYLE

A poet's style is composed of all the characteristics of his verse. Hence, the word is often used to describe the particular verbal effects the poet makes, the sort of words he chooses, and the way he puts them together for reasons not entirely connected with their meaning. This is also called 'poetic diction'. It is a difficult subject to write about, because to identify features of style does not necessarily add anything to the reader's appreciation. It is like saying of a painting that it is 22″ by 34″ and painted in gold, black and vermilion. The subject of style also involves us in the difficult question whether the sounds of words can be beautiful in themselves, or only in association with the sense or suggestion of the words. Nevertheless, it will be worth while to identify broadly some features of Eliot's style because the exercise brings out the variety of his command over words.

He is for the most part direct and conversational. He adopts the language of one educated person talking to another. He drops from time to time into a more fragmented utterance as if he is thinking to himself, while at other times he heightens his style to produce a more incantatory effect. He writes in various modes of dramatic speech and of parody, and he makes regular use of the formal artifices of style such as alliteration, repetition, internal rhyme, assonance, and play on words to enrich the texture of his verse.

Gerontion typifies the conversational style. He is peevish as he draws out the opening picture, but he is quite straightforward. We may not know what it's all about, but we have no difficulty in understanding what he is saying:

> Here I am, an old man in a dry month,
> Being read to by a boy, waiting for rain.
> I was neither at the hot gates
> Nor fought in the warm rain
> Nor knee deep in the salt marsh, heaving a cutlass,

Marie, also in Part I of *The Waste Land*, a little bored:

> Summer surprised us, coming over the Starnbergersee
> With a shower of rain; we stopped in the colonnade,
> And went on in sunlight, into the Hofgarten,
> And drank coffee, and talked for an hour.

8–11

The observer in *The Waste Land* is just as direct. He is a little meditative, but except for the metaphorical use of death in the fourth line, the language is very straightforward:

> Unreal City
> Under the brown fog of a winter dawn,
> A crowd flowed over London Bridge, so many,
> I had not thought death had undone so many.
> Sighs, short and infrequent, were exhaled,
> And each man fixed his eyes before his feet.

60–5

In *Ash Wednesday*, the picture in Part III is expressed with an equally direct simplicity, a pastoral scene, spied through a window on a staircase:

> At the first turning of the third stair
> Was a slotted window bellied like the fig's fruit
> And beyond the hawthorn blossom and a pasture scene
> The broadbacked figure drest in blue and green
> Enchanted the maytime with an antique flute.

In this simple style, Eliot is most strongly restoring to poetry the common idiom which is important to it, and which had to some extent been lost by the poets of the late 19th century. (This has been made too much of at times, for their greater lack was in what they chose to write about rather than just in their vocabulary.)

Eliot can vary this manner a little according to the character of the speaker. The lady in the *Portrait* is somewhat archly hesitant in her delivery:

> 'You do not know how much they mean to me, my friends,
> And how, how rare and strange it is, to find
> In a life composed so much, so much of odds and ends,
> (For indeed I do not love it . . . you knew? you are not blind!
> How keen you are!)
> To find a friend who has these qualities,
> Who has, and gives
> Those qualities upon which friendship lives.'

In the first three lines she repeats words as she seeks the right phrase for her meaning, and then never achieves anything beyond a platitude, though she is charming for all that. And there is a tiny affectation, a mannerism in her employment of the word 'keen' (in the sense of 'keen of perception', 'sympathetic'). You can almost hear her draw the word out.

Quite another kind of person is to be found in Section II of *The Waste Land*: the barmaid:

> When Lil's husband got demobbed, I said—
> I didn't mince my words, I said to her myself,
> HURRY UP PLEASE IT'S TIME

Now Albert's coming back, make yourself a bit smart.
He'll want to know what you done with that money he gave you
To get yourself some teeth. He did, I was there.
You have them all out, Lil, and get a nice set,
He said, I swear, I can't bear to look at you.

139-46

and she goes on in one of Eliot's finest pieces of dramatic and humorous writing. Her repeated 'I said' is very far from the delicate archness of the lady in the *Portrait*, but a mannerism none the less, a meaningless habit.

Building on his command of the conversational and direct, Eliot heightens his style a little when he wishes to make some more central statement. Here is Gerontion again:

I would meet you upon this honestly.
I that was near your heart was removed therefrom
To lose beauty in terror, terror in inquisition.
I have lost my passion: why should I need to keep it
Since what is kept must be adulterated?
I have lost my sight, smell, hearing, taste and touch:
How should I use them for your closer contact?

There is something rather *proper* in the opening 'I would meet'. It is more formal than what you might expect—for instance, 'I want to meet', or 'I would like to meet you'—and there is a similar kind of formality in the use of 'therefrom'. Also the last four lines of the extract show a balanced pattern of a statement followed by a question implying a comment on the statement.

There is formal writing in *The Waste Land* too, in Part I:

What are the roots that clutch, what branches grow
Out of this stony rubbish? Son of man,
You cannot say, or guess, for you know only
A heap of broken images, where the sun beats,
And the dead tree gives no shelter, the cricket no relief,
And the dry stone no sound of water.

19-24

Here is the rhetorical question, heightened in effect still more by its paired opening—'What are the roots . . . what branches grow'. And then the formal address, 'Son of man', and the triplet of phrases at the end of the extract. In *Ash Wednesday* the formality is that of prayer, and in the *Four Quartets* it is, as with the metre, a kind of measured and achieved balance between conversation and address.

Eliot varies his style with parody. In *A Game of Chess* (Part II of *The Waste Land*), he opens with a line almost straight out of *Antony and Cleopatra:*

The Chair she sat in, like a burnished throne,

—but then somewhat disarmingly proceeds in the manner of Milton which he keeps up intermittently for twenty lines, effectively mocking the powdered and jewel-bedecked woman in her preposterous room. Another instance of parody is in *Sweeney Erect*, though perhaps parody is the wrong word, because no other writer's style is directly imitated here. The style in the opening verses of this poem is, however, savagely inflated, almost grotesquely so, in view of what follows. We are asked in portentous language to imagine a remote and wild region, a shore on the Aegean; the adjectives are chosen to create the inflated effect: 'cavernous waste', 'unstilled', 'bold anfractuous', 'snarled and yelping'. In the next verse, we learn that it is to be no more than a picture, one of those pictures with portraits of gods puffing to make the winds drawn in the sky. The temperature drops a little, though the gales are still insurgent, and we remember the story of Ariadne, who, deserted by Theseus after she had helped him to escape from the Labyrinth, later married Dionysus and became a goddess of fertility, and a symbol of spring. Then finally in the third stanza we drop to a much more restricted picture, a sordid room in the morning after an even more sordid and barren sexual affair between Sweeney, who like Grishkin represents human nature reduced to and in some aspects below animal nature, and an unknown woman, an epileptic, whom he has seduced. He is thoroughly complacent about the whole thing, including her fit, for he 'knows the female temperament' and so proceeds with his shaving, having relieved his conscience with that facile delusion, and the ladies of the corridor are only concerned with the propriety of the whole affair. Only Doris manages to take action, and the 'But' in the last stanza implies that Eliot approves this much at least, though her action is nothing more than to provide the same sops that she would require herself in similar circumstances. The whole situation is one of crass ignorance, snobbery, insensitivity, degradation, and denial of human nature, and the poem is one of Eliot's most savage. The epigraph, which is taken, appropriately, from *The Maid's Tragedy* by Beaumont and Fletcher, speaks equally appropriately of a desolation behind the immediate scene, and that is all we see behind this wretched collection of unfortunates. This is the position human nature has reached, this is history, this is what the ape-man has 'progressed' to. And thus it is savagely that Eliot opens the poem with the ironic references to classical settings and classical myths. It is as much as to say, 'Just do that, do paint me these things, and then I will show you the details we will put in the picture'. And many of the best effects of the poem are created by the choice and positioning of words. The fourth stanza is made the more vicious, both by the contrast between the fertility reference in Ariadne and the 'withered root', and also, indeed more so, by the combined harshness of the sound effects. Words like 'knots' and 'slitted' and 'gashed' and 'cropped' and 'sickle' combine with the sense to stress the somewhat bitter experience. I do not think, however, that Eliot is bitter. The whole poem has the same kind of ironic detachment discovered in *Whispers of Immortality*, as may be seen from the stanza which introduces Sweeney:

Sweeney addressed full length to shave
Broadbottomed, pink from nape to base,

The word 'addressed' is used with the same sort of reference as when a golfer addresses a ball before hitting it, and in the choice of this rather special word the poet demonstrates his ability to move on from the epileptic to contemplate sardonically the portrait of Sweeney, who, for all his degraded human nature, is never treated with disdain. Similarly the ladies of the corridor are rather a subject for our mirth than our scorn. It is not easy to demonstrate how these effects are created, and they are perhaps finally dependent on familiarity with the tone of the whole collection of *Poems 1920*.

It is easy to find instances of Eliot's use of the traditional poetic devices; it is hard to say exactly what the effect of them is. Prufrock says:

In a minute there is time
For decisions and revisions which a minute will reverse.

These lines contain assonance: they are dominated by the short 'i' sound, and conclude neatly on a new vowel sound while preserving a consonant pattern from earlier in the line ('revisions' . . . 'reverse'). Clearly these details contribute to the effect of the lines, give additional pleasure. The difficult question is whether in so doing they enrich the line arbitrarily, or by adding to the meaning or suggestive power of the line. In this case it seems that together with the rhythm, the effects imply the monotony of the activity described and its littleness. Decisions which ought to be important things become nothing more than the ticks of a clock.

There is a similar passage in *Gerontion*, dealing with the same activity, and the same vowel sound is dominant:

These with a thousand small deliberations
Protract the profit of their chilled delirium.

though the lines are less feverish, as Gerontion is on the whole less agitated. But what more can be said of the line: 'Protract the profit of their chilled delirium' where it is possible to identify alliteration at first, then assonance, with the final word picking up the 'r' from the earlier words? The line is finely shaped; it has in itself a pleasing formal quality. Is it then because at this point in the poem Gerontion is forming a sort of conclusion for which he would wish to use carefully finished language? These are delicate problems, about which, since people respond very differently to the sounds of words, it is impossible to be at all final. The care with which Eliot fashions his verse is, however, enough to make us look very carefully at the shape and sound of every line because we may well discover there some indication of the way it is to be read.

Occasionally, as in the Choruses from *The Rock*, Eliot uses a much more obvious rhetoric, using techniques characteristic of formal classical or medieval rhetoric. A forceful series of questions:

> Where is the Life we have lost in living?
> Where is the wisdom we have lost in knowledge?
> Where is the knowledge we have lost in information?

Or a formal repetition:

> I have given you hands which you turn from worship,
> I have given you speech, for endless palaver,
> I have given you my Law, and you set up commissions,

and so on for a passage of six lines. These are formal effects suited to the occasion of a pageant in which 'grand' verse is appropriate. There are other occasions when the manipulating of words is obvious to create a sense of paradox, or of an idea which is not clear. So, again from *The Rock*, Chorus VII:

> Then came, at a predetermined moment, a moment in time and of time,
> A moment not out of time, but in time, in what we call history: transecting, bisecting the world of time, a moment in time but not like a moment of time,
> A moment in time but time was made through that moment: for without the meaning there is no time, and that moment of time gave the meaning.

The arrangement of words in itself represents the striving towards the idea. This is even more prominent in *Ash Wednesday*, Part V:

> If the lost word is lost, if the spent word is spent
> If the unheard, unspoken
> Word is unspoken, unheard;
> Still is the unspoken word, the Word unheard,
> The Word without a word, the Word within
> The world and for the world;
> And the light shone in darkness and
> Against the Word the unstilled world still whirled
> About the centre of the silent Word.

This is hard. It is also made deliberately harder by the poet, for he is trying to express the inscrutability of the concept he is describing.

It would be possible to multiply examples of Eliot's handling of words to show what he can do with them. Most cases are unique, and appropriate to their context. The important thing is to observe the possibilities.

7

Poetry: 1909–1930

The subjects of Eliot's poems, although various, are not very often like the subject matter of earlier poetry. He does not describe the beauties of nature, or only by means of hints and allusions. Equally he does not often use love as a central subject for his poetry, though he is very much concerned with it. His poems are, like Browning's, about human nature, but where Browning is deeply interested in individual idiosyncrasies, Eliot is more interested in the race. His characters are seldom most interesting because of what they are as individuals, but because of what they are as representatives of mankind in general. And as his poetry develops, he becomes more and more an exclusively religious poet. The characters fade until in *Ash Wednesday* and the *Four Quartets* there appear only the poet himself as 'I' and the occasional shadowy figures without names, such as the lady and the flute-player in *Ash Wednesday*, and the even more remote figures in the *Four Quartets*, voices only sometimes: the children, dancers, public men in *East Coker*, the shadowy figure whom the poet meets in *Little Gidding*. By now, he is entirely concerned with the general aspects of human nature.

'PRUFROCK AND OTHER OBSERVATIONS' (1917)

Eliot's first collection of poems has a much greater consistency than his second, though the second has on the whole a single tone. The first collection is full of characters, who are as interesting in themselves as they are as representatives, though they are more important as the latter. We have Prufrock himself, the lady (a society lady this one, rather like those whom Prufrock sets out to visit), Cousin Harriet, Cousin Nancy, and Aunt Helen,

Mr. Apollinax, and the girl of *La Figlia che Piange*. The mood of the collection is set by the first poem. We are in a town, frequently indeed actually in the streets, which are not very pleasant. We are among a society of some distinction. The people are educated, sometimes highly sophisticated, over-subtle in their relationships so as to be decadent; and if they are not that, then they respect conventional proprieties to an extent that makes them negative. They are perhaps a little underhand, and perhaps a little foolish, though we must deduce all these characteristics from passing hints. They are objects of satire, but it is not that ferocious satire that Pope could produce, because Eliot is not angry; he is pitying and smiling in places, but he is too much among these people and this society himself to be really biting, and it is the mixture of attitudes in the more serious poems that is the keynote of this book. The poet is at one moment cynical, at another generous and idealistic. This is to be seen in *La Figlia che Piange*, but it is perhaps most clear in the last of the *Preludes*. Already as early as this, Eliot has shown his sense of the common nature of music and poetry by titling this poem *Preludes*. I take this as one poem, not only because it is set out as one in the book, nor because it is Eliot's manner to construct a poem out of a number of loosely connected sections, but because each section leads up to the final one. The poem is a series of descriptive variations based on details of a town scene, a winter evening, wet, dirty, with unpleasant smells in the air; a morning, the next perhaps, still dingy, nasty, dull and monotonous; the morning again when you don't want to get up and when you reflect on dreams, still sordid and soiled, the 'you' here being a woman. Finally evening again, still dull and monotonous. It is the watcher of these scenes whose soul is 'stretched tight across the skies', as much as to say his soul takes them all in, and is stretched as far as it can go by them. And then the 'His' changes to 'I' (this technique is common in this volume; Prufrock is probably speaking to himself, and the speaker of *La Figlia che Piange* sees himself outside himself) and the speaker of the poem concludes:

> I am moved by fancies that are curled
> Around these images, and cling:

> The notion of some infinitely gentle
> Infinitely suffering thing.

Thus despite the sequence of images which depicts the scenes as nasty, grimy, and squalid, there remains this perception of something deeper and far better, buried beneath the monotony and dirt. It is this sort of redemption of the things he is describing that leads one to a conviction of Eliot's deep humanity, even though he tosses this perception away immediately with the next lines:

> Wipe your hand across your mouth, and laugh;
> The worlds revolve like ancient women
> Gathering fuel in vacant lots.

Dash it away, this absurd degrading suggestion that there is anything good to be discovered in these worlds of the town; laugh at it, it is as futile as the plight of the destitute old woman who must glean for fuel in derelict building-sites. There remains, though, in the very choice of this image the same ambiguity as the whole poem conveys. An old woman searching for fuel is more likely to arouse our pity for helplessness and loneliness than our scorn or derision.

Some of the poems in this first collection seem to be little more than a craftsman's exercises. *Rhapsody on a Windy Night* is another town scene, and another poem based on a musical idea: a rhapsody suggests 'a composition of enthusiastic character but indefinite form'. The rhapsodic effect of this poem is discovered in sequences like:

> Half-past three,
> The lamp sputtered,
> The lamp muttered in the dark.
> The lamp hummed:
> 'Regard the moon,
> La lune ne garde aucune rancune,
> She winks a feeble eye,
> She smiles into corners.
> She smooths the hair of the grass.
> The moon has lost her memory,
> A washed out smallpox cracks her face,
> Her hand twists a paper rose,

> That smells of dust and eau de Cologne,
> She is alone
> With all the old nocturnal smells
> That cross and cross across her brain.'

The basis of the poem is that on a moonlit night the speaker walks down a street in which the street-lamps eventually dominate his walk so much as to act as triggers to series of fanciful and disorganised imaginings. The poem takes a sort of playful delight in word patterns and strings of ideas without their certainly meaning anything. Thus the three lines that begin with 'The lamp. . .' convey a mock dramatic effect; also the excursion into French for 'the moon has no grudge' where one might be expected to linger almost jocularly on the repeated '-une' sound. Then the personification of the moon here is exaggerated; we are not to take it very seriously. The moon is like an old silly woman, living on her memories, senile and pathetic, but not in this case arousing our pity because she is, after all, the moon and we do not feel really sorry for the moon, even personified, except a sort of mock sorrow, a game. Finally in the extract quoted, the repetition in the line 'That cross and cross across her brain'.

This poem is not entirely a game. There are images in it which share some of the effects in *Preludes* and elsewhere. The woman with the border of her dress torn—she has been involved in some sordid sexual encounter, we suppose—the cat eating rancid butter, the female smells in shuttered rooms, and the last twist of the knife. But the overall effect is played down by the shape and manner of the poem; the rhymes are in a way too obvious. We are meant to think that the poet found butter to rhyme with gutter and so created that passage, and similarly though ambiguously in the last two lines, the lamp says, among other things,

> 'Put your shoes at the door, sleep, prepare for life.'
> The last twist of the knife.

We might almost have expected *knife* to rhyme with *life*, and thus the effect is ironical both ways. 'Life' indeed. Whatever would I be doing preparing for that, for heaven's sake? That is one's first reaction. But then because of the jingle, we wonder if the ironical comment isn't made with a self-denying smile, too. (It is like some of the Fool's comments in *King Lear*: too easy, too facile, too often word jingles.)

Eliot is not often credited with a sense of humour in his major works, but he certainly displays that faculty in this and the second book of poems. His humour is never open, never obvious, and never easy. It is always revealed through irony, and irony is the most inaccessible type of humour. In Eliot's hands, it is a matter of not revealing whether he means the reader to sympathise or not. It is also the most difficult type of humour to write about, because as soon as you attempt to demonstrate its presence, it vanishes away. It is best revealed in Eliot in the more caustic and less gentle poems in the second volume, but it is also present here in, for example, *The Boston Evening Transcript*. Here we move away from the sordidly urban, though the poet is not likely to find any 'infinitely gentle, infinitely suffering thing' in the confines of Boston, where he found propriety and gentility even more offensive than squalor. The image of ripe corn for the readers of the *Transcript* is not perhaps the best one, for we are surely not meant to take anything from the simile except the swaying, whereas we might well be tempted to link up the richness and beauty of the corn with the same readers, which would give quite another effect. The ironical effect is present in the matter-of-fact way in which the poem is presented. We hardly know whether we are meant to approve or disapprove of anything referred to, until we reach the poet's weariness, and then we see that there is some sharpness in the words:

> When evening quickens faintly in the street,
> Wakening the appetites of life in some
> And to others bringing the *Boston Evening Transcript*.

Neither arrival is better. 'The appetites of life' refers to no more than the sexual appetites which are aroused as night draws on, and the *Boston Evening Transcript* feeds the appetites of death, of negation; and the final irony is that the poet is confessedly a party to these appetites of death, for he has fetched the paper and brought it to Cousin Harriet.

It is these two poems which raise the effect of this first collection to greater seriousness. They set the tone on which the other slighter poems depend, in the same way as *Gerontion* does for the second collection. *Prufrock* is a dramatic monologue. We have to imagine a character speaking the lines, and a context in which he speaks them. The context is not absolutely clear, though its broad outlines are obvious enough. The man is going to a sophisticated party, apparently a ladies' occasion of a cultural kind, but one which shares the vacuity of Boston society already examined in other poems. The refrain couplet about these ladies, 'talking of Michelangelo', has an empty jingling quality. Prufrock, however, has a special mission, for he is in love with one of the ladies and is going to declare it. But he is an irresolute person for whom the simplest decision is a matter of strain, speculation and distress. Whatever he says to the lady may lead to an irrevocable step taken into the future for which he must bear the responsibility. This is why he asks: 'Do I dare disturb the universe?', for any action which changes the pattern of things 'disturbs the universe'. And since he does not know where he is going in universal terms, how can he take that responsibility?

The poem begins with a quotation from Dante's *Inferno* (translated here by D. Sayers):

> If I thought that I were making
> Answer to one that might return to view
> The world, this flame should evermore cease shaking.
>
> But since from this abyss, if I hear true,
> None ever came alive, I have no fear
> Of infamy, but give thee answer due.

XXVII 61–6

Dante has encountered in Hell a character called Guido da Montefeltro who asks him for news of Italy, which Dante gives. Then he is asked in return to disclose what has brought him to Hell, which he agrees to do, though only on the assumption that Dante is another lost soul who will never return to tell of Guido's shame. The epigraph suggests, then, a confession, but one in which there is something which ought to be hidden from us.

Then the narrator goes on his way. The poem follows a sort of action. Prufrock goes towards the room where the women are, imagining the experience before him. He reaches it, in imagination, and comes away without having done what he set out to do. He is clearly a failure. He is not Lazarus come back from the dead with some great explanation. Nor is he Hamlet, who for all his indecision took some action and some responsibility. He has no heroic quality. He does not dare disturb the universe, and falls back into trivial speculations whether he shall eat a peach or part his hair behind. He escapes into a fantasy world of unreal love, with mermaids, for this is all he can ever achieve.

There is in the first half of the poem some hope of success. The sense of failure does not begin until the sections which start: 'And would it have been worth it after all'. By this time he has seen himself enter the salon, take tea, fail to ask his question, and seen the footman 'snicker' in a superior way, or at least imagined that, and he has come away, afraid to take the positive step which would have made him 'great' just because it was a step which would have changed something. He knows, all the while he pursues this meditation, that he is doomed to failure, and he lets this out abruptly and touchingly in those lines which appear to be completely inconsequential:

> I should have been a pair of ragged claws
> Scuttling across the floors of silent seas.

He is no better suited to cope with human experiences than a crab. He cannot cope especially with 'human voices'. When experience reaches the stage of communication he is lost, hence the preference for 'silent seas'; and hence at the end of the poem his drowning when awakened from his reverie by 'human voices'.

It is most important to follow the mood of this poem, called up by the images first of all, of dullness, drabness, negation, ageing, purposelessness, and then by the manner of the deliberations, which repeat themselves insistently without ever getting anywhere. Prufrock is a less desiccated Gerontion (see pp. 55–6).

It is also most important to enter into some sort of imaginative sympathy with him, to follow the way his thinking goes. Prufrock is not being described. He is in action before us, and he needs the kind of approach that we would give to a character in a play. His overwhelming question is most likely: 'Where are we going, and why?', though he never gets round to asking it, and, as Guido in Hell wished, the heart of the matter is never reported for us. However, this is not at all the most important subject of the poem. It is of no great consequence what Prufrock says. It matters very much what sort of person he is, and *how* he says what he says.

Portrait of a Lady belongs in very much the same social atmosphere as *The Love Song*, a sophisticated atmosphere of leisure, bored, speculative, inconclusive, though this poem lacks the tendency towards bitterness which is implied by the Prufrock poem. This time the satire is chiefly directed at the lady, one of those ladies whom Prufrock was going to visit, though it would not be wise to read this poem as a straightforward sequel to the first poem, nor as another way of looking at Prufrock's situation, this time from the lady's point of view. In some ways, this second poem is more characteristic of Eliot's earliest writing than *The Love Song*. It has the same bitter-sweet quality of *Conversation Galante* and *La Figlia che Piange*, where the satirical viewpoint is only there as a defence against recognising the pain of the situation. *Portrait of a Lady* tells of a relationship between a man and a woman—the woman older, experienced in the ways of her sophisticated society, affected; the man younger, inexperienced, but with pretensions to enter that society, while recognising it from time to time for what it is, empty. The affair lasts for a year, and ends in the young man's departure abroad, wondering what it has meant. The epigraph suggests this uncertainty. He has committed—well, what has he committed, but anyway, that was in another country, he is abroad now, and it is all forgotten. It is just possible that we are meant to take it from the epigraph that the young man has played the gigolo to the older woman, who has since died, for she is one 'about to reach her journey's end'; though that would be an unusually obvious reading of an epigraph in Eliot, who normally uses them only to suggest something about the poem.

The sharpness of the poem lies in the representation of the words spoken by the lady, which suggest very clearly her fatigued affectation, her clinging to experience, her searching for 'friends'. This word covers that pain she would feel if she had to express her longing in any more direct way. Her 'friendships' are all her life. So strong is this attitude, that she thinks Chopin's soul should be resurrected among two or three friends. To have him sent to any common Heaven, amid all the ranks of the blessed, would be too overpowering, too coarse. Her world is one where you must strain to catch the meaning of what is being said, where communication is all by innuendoes. After a while, the young man becomes aware of a definite 'false note', though his life is not much fuller, or more significant, since he lets time pass in trivial occupations reminiscent of Prufrock's coffee-spoons.

In Section II it is spring. The lady drones on with her memories, and her worldly wisdom. He is bored, and yet he wishes somehow to make amends for what she says to him. She has said he is young and strong and has the future to come, whereas her life is ending. The sense of fatigue and boredom is very strong in this section, though there is poignancy in the question how the young can make amends to the old for being young. In Section III it is autumn, and the young man is going abroad. He is anxious, for he does not know how she will take the news. She begins by suggesting a correspondence, and he is pleased, perhaps because this would mean their affair was slightly less pointless, but she pulls his pleasure away at once when she says they did not become 'friends'. At this he feels lost. What does she mean? Why did they not? He is frightened by seeing how inadequately two people communicate. He is left with no idea how he is to interpret the experience, nor who has the best of it, nor whether he has understood.

In the case of Prufrock, it is fairly clear what we should feel towards him; we are sympathetic with his sufferings, though we do not admire him. It is much the same thing with the lady in this poem. Less obviously, we also do not admire the young man, whose pretensions to take part intimately in the lady's society are as affected as is that society itself, and whose 'interpretations' of the situation are equally pretentious. He is less clearly imagined than the other two characters, however, and it is not always clear that we are meant to remain as detached from him as from the others.

These two poems are the most important in the collection, because even though they are 'dramatic'—that is, they express a specific and unique situation for unique characters, and we shall feel very little about them unless we approach them that way— those characters do take on a symbolic significance, and that is why we retain sympathy for them. For all their fecklessness, they are human all the same, and their problems, attenuated and super-subtle as they may be, are a reflection of anybody's doubts and problems in human relationships and in wondering about reality and responsibility.

The subject of the first collection is a society of which the details are frequently sordid, of which various aspects are deaden-ingly proper with undertones of hypocrisy, and in which the relationships between men and women are so sophisticated as to be dissociated from anything positive, lasting, and satisfying, although the poet himself still finds occasion to wonder, and is not, despite his inclinations, altogether given over to cynicism. The only other kind of sexual relationships are coarse, uncouth, and animal, and are fit only for cynicism or disgust. It is this theme chiefly which is developed in the second collection where there is even less to redeem the society which Eliot is inspecting than there was in the first.

Finally, the most revealing detail of the book, revealing of Eliot's purpose, is the epigraph taken from *Il Purgatorio*, the second part of Dante's *Divina Commedia*, which is translated:

> Now thou'lt know
> How large and warm my love about thee clings,
> When I forget our nothingness, and go
> Treating these shadows like material things

> XXI 133–6

We have no need to know the context of these words to understand that we are to see in them Eliot's love of life, even these examples of it, and his treatment of them as material things even though they are no more substantial than the shades that people Dante's worlds.

'POEMS 1920'

Gerontion is not typical of the poems in this collection. It is rather an extension of the first two poems of the first collection. Gerontion might well be an elder version of Prufrock, with his understanding of the vanity of things, a tougher Prufrock, but nevertheless a man who can contemplate and pursue 'a thousand small deliberations'—a good phrase in itself to describe what Prufrock is doing. I have already discussed some aspects of the poem *Gerontion* (pp. 55–6); here I will only recall its main topics. It concerns an old man who, although he sees no hope, and no solution to the inexhaustible problems that human experience presents, nevertheless is able to conclude bleakly that time goes on, and we have not got to the end yet. This picture of old age is the bleakest poem that Eliot has so far written, for it states very clearly that the senses have failed and the mind remains no more than a means to excitement to pass the time. It also states that heroism and other such noble virtuous qualities and characteristics are nothing but vanity. (This marks a development from Prufrock, where although he was no hero, others still might be.) It implies, too, that the sign from God which is to provide an answer, at least to show God is there, has been dissipated in vanity and frivolity. Christ, who came in a metaphorical spring like a metaphorical tiger, with all the vitality of both, has been fragmented until he is as meaningless as the 'vacant shuttles' which 'weave the wind'. The shuttles have no wool on them, nor is there any substance in the warp.

Nevertheless, Gerontion comes on to say:

> The tiger springs in the new year. Us he devours. Think at last
> We have not reached conclusion, when I
> Stiffen in a rented house. Think at last
> I have not made this show purposelessly . . .

In the face of all the bleak conclusions, Gerontion does not approach despair. He is a part of things, and that is enough. He is like the fractured atoms of the people he has mentioned, now flung out into the galaxy, or a gull in the wind, anywhere in the world, its feathers strewn by that wind, the process of fragmentation, the fracturing already begun, though the winds so far have done no more than drive him into a sleepy corner. There are some important topics raised in this poem. It is the first to adopt a specifically religious way of thinking, and the first to introduce at some depth Eliot's special preoccupation, the passing of time and what that really means, the importance of what we call things temporal, and the nature of things eternal. When you consider that the atoms we are made of are nearly indestructible, in what sense then do we die? Or, another approach, when you consider that the atoms of which we are made are continually replaced, in what sense then are we ever ourselves? These and countless similar questions confront any person in an age as scientifically aware as the present one, and they are the sort of questions implicit already in this poem. In later poems we become involved in even more difficult, or at least disturbing, questions concerning the nature of time.

The general aspects of the view of human nature in the rest of this book are unpleasant, and largely unredeemed except by the sharp irony of the surface. Most obviously, the poems are shot through with images which present sex as utterly degraded, a matter of seduction, or of worse than animal indulgence, bestial or commercial. There is Princess Volupine in *Burbank with a Baedeker: Bleistein with a Cigar* who is, as her name vividly suggests, both vulpine and voluptuous. She will accept the attentions of the rich visitors to Venice, so long as it pays her to, and she knows how to get the ones that will pay. One of her possible suitors, Bleistein, is presented as an amphibious creature, a frog or a toad, staring from the slime of prehistoric times. There is Grishkin, whom we have met, and her very close relation, Rachel *née* Rabinovitch, who 'tears at the grapes with murderous paws' in *Sweeney Among the Nightingales*. And most enormous, in every sense of that word, there is Sweeney himself, apelike, and associated with other animals, called Sweeney Erect, the ape on its hind legs, and perhaps more. And all this, too, associated with disease: Volupine has a 'phthisic hand'—she has tuberculosis; Sweeney's mate is an epileptic. The picture is altogether nasty. But this is by no means the only degradation in human society. Volupine's Venice is undermined with financial corruption:

> The rats are underneath the piles.
> The Jew is underneath the lot.

The visitors to Venice now are the money-makers: Bleistein, Sir Ferdinand Klein, and Burbank, too, no doubt, though he has some finer discrimination. We have already seen the debasement of human nature in *Sweeney Erect* (pp. 77–9). The picture continues to deteriorate.

There is, however, by no means the same overall effect from this set of poems. The general view is nasty, but it does not ever quite grow into a coherent view. The final effect of each poem is too distinct from any of the others for us to find an overall pattern. Apart from the nastiness I have described, the 'meaning' of the individual poems belongs exclusively to each one. And this would coincide with our view of the tight, concise form of these poems. *Burbank* is a portrait of Venice showing that human nature is degraded. *Sweeney Erect* is a more intimate portrait of a 'domestic' scene showing the same thing. *A Cooking Egg*, that is an egg which has just gone off and is therefore not fit to eat direct, depicts a sort of castrated society given over to scones and crumpets, and also makes fun of the conventional view of Heaven. *The Hippopotamus* laughs at the Church, the so-called True Church, which is not true at all. *Whispers of Immortality*, although it pursues the idea of degradation, is less easy to pin down briefly. *Mr. Eliot's Sunday Morning Service* also strikes at the Church in its deteriorated state. (We might at this point recall the degradation of Christ the tiger in *Gerontion*.) *Sweeney Among the Nightingales* is concerned with the loss of heroism. Not one of these poems is easy of interpretation, both on account of their compression, their difficult vocabulary, and their often concealed ideas, and they represent Eliot at his most abstruse. It is interesting to note that the first title of this collection was '*Ara vos prec*', which is a quotation again from '*Il Purgatorio*', meaning 'Now I pray you'. It is the beginning of a speech by a poet, Arnaut Daniel, which goes on to request Dante to spare a thought for him, as he proceeds up the mountain of Purgatory.

Although this is a less consistent collection of poems, its general drift might be to persuade us to spare a thought for a sorry picture of human life, both in its individual and social aspects.

'THE WASTE LAND'

Once you have come to terms with the technique of this poem, discussed on pp. 65–8, it is by no means the most difficult of Eliot's poems. It has a fairly obvious development, and the images are not difficult to interpret. It is linguistically very much clearer and probably more enjoyable than anything in *Poems 1920*. To help us towards an understanding, we need to realise that all wars are one war, all battles one battle, all journeys one journey, all rivers one river, all rooms one room, all loves one love, indeed ultimately all people one person, so that all the specific examples of these things in the poem are in every case representative of their kind.

Here is a short analysis of the poem in which I have by no means drawn out all the implications of each line, which are often numerous. Some have already been mentioned in the discussion of the technique. I have tried here to keep the general shape of the poem in sight. It may be helpful to remember the party game of Consequences in this connection, though I do no more than hazard the suggestion which came to me from the title of the last section, *What the Thunder Said*. In the game, you first of all write down the place where the experience to follow occurred, then what he said to her, and what she said to him. Then the last two titles are 'And the Consequence was' and 'And the World said'. Each person starts with a piece of paper on which he writes down a place. He then folds over the piece he has written on and passes the paper round for the next person to fill in the next section, and so on until all the sections are completed. When the last section has been filled in, everyone unravels their piece of paper and reads out the result, which can be hilarious or futile as chance decrees. In this poem, given Eliot's attitude to the coming together of sections of a poem until they make a whole, each section might have been written by a different person as in the game, and the pattern of the poem faintly echoes the game, too. The first three sections are concerned with the time ('All time'), the place ('the Waste Land'), the people and what they say to each other. The consequence is 'Death by Water', and the thunder says 'Datta, Dayadhvam, Damyata'.

In *The Burial of the Dead*, there are four pictures. The first two are introduced by two setting passages, which also introduce the waste land. Because the land is waste, spring is painful to it. Spring stirs it into life when it has dropped into forgetfulness under the snow. Here the setting is made peculiarly painful by the choice of lilacs, which, like hyacinths in the second picture, are flowers of peculiar intensity. They are brightly coloured and strongly scented, and of the sort of size and shape that the eye cannot evade, and they, like hyacinths, look and smell best after a shower, and so the contrast with the dead land is acute. We, the people of the waste land, the poet, the speaker, you, me, would rather sleep away through the winter, dull, and warm, and dried, a little life. Then Marie's life which is little, too, an example of one of us, in the waste land. Then the poet grows rougher and more dramatic in his delivery. We are 'stony rubbish', for we have rejected spring and life in favour of a 'heap of broken images', and the waste land is no longer just that of winter, but is become a desert, where there is drought, and death and a burning sun, and just a little shadow where the poet can find life enough to show you and us a fearful vision of a desolate land. Then abruptly to the hyacinth garden and the love affair which leads to nothing but desolation (see pp. 62–3, 66–7). Both these pictures are poignant because they have in them things and associations which we recognise as beautiful, and this is what is fearful because these things are buried in the waste; they are like dead things. Madame Sosostris and the crowd of people in London are more obviously features of the waste land. Madame Sosostris undertakes the vanity of fortune-telling, and the crowd has been undone by death. At the same time, these two episodes have something behind them which is frightening; they are not simply what should be alive buried, they have a sort of eerie life. Even though Madame Sosostris is ill, she can still see into the cards, and she does foresee things which will happen later in the poem. She sees Phlebas, and the lady of situations whom we meet in Part II. She sees Mr. Eumenides of Part III and the crowds of Part IV and she looks forward to the time when we shall see that we and Phlebas are not very different, and that we shall very likely share his fate. Nevertheless, she belongs in the land of monotony, like her friend Mrs. Equitone, and in a land of suspicion, where 'one must be so careful'. She, like Marie and all the others, is European, and if there are boundaries to the waste land they may be those of Europe; but there is no special reason to see it as being limited in this way. The Unreal City is London, but might be any. We are back in winter now, no longer in the desert, and the death is that of the commuters crossing London Bridge, a sight which must be far more terrifying now than it was when Eliot wrote the poem. The line: 'I had not thought death had undone so many' is a translation of another piece from Dante, this time from the *Inferno*. Before Dante enters Hell proper, he passes through a sort of antechamber where he encounters the spirits of those who have lived futile lives because they have been unable to make any real choice of a way of life. They have been entirely negative. These people have no hope of anything ever happening to them, and this is almost worse than the punishment of Hell itself, to be regarded as utterly negative. In the next line, by means of a note, though hardly obviously in the text, the waste land becomes the first circle of Hell itself, known as Limbo, where reside the pagans and the unbaptised who could not have entered into God's grace anyway, whether they had wished it or not. There they reside, untormented, but eternally conscious of their loss. The passage that Eliot refers us to is this:

> We heard no loud complaint, no crying here,
> No sound of grief except the sound of sighing
> Quivering for ever through the eternal air.

IV, 25-7

Throughout this section are hints and statements of death as something dull and negative. A preference for winter, life as memory, neither living nor dead, death by water, undone by death, and the corpse: this sequence of ideas and images becomes more direct and obvious as the poem proceeds. Also, as the poem proceeds, the hints of something poignant, something beautiful which might redeem this negative life a little, become reduced until they are no more than short and infrequent sighs.

As soon as we move into *A Game of Chess* we are in a world unredeemed, a world of death, a waste land which has rejected the spring. The two women both belong in these worlds; the first is bored, she cannot think of anything to do, for all the splendour of her surroundings, which show among other things the sordid rape of Philomel by Tereus, which Eliot manages to make peculiarly nasty with ' "Jug Jug" to dirty ears'. The nightingales sing in vain. The lady can only think of crazy things to do, like rushing out into the street with her hair down, and however much she shuts her eyes she and her companion, who is more prone to face the truth, can never shut out the desert sun of their waste land.

The barmaid and Lil inhabit an equally awful world. The barmaid tells Lil to smarten herself up in order to be able to give her husband, who is coming back from the war, a good time and there is not much doubt what sort of good time Lil is expected to give. Lil, at the same time, has rejected the object of marriage, which is reproduction. She has had five children by the way, as it were without knowing what she was doing, and now she has forced an abortion on herself although it has done her no good in other respects. There is some bite in the question: 'What you get married for if you don't want children?' And interspersed in this scene is the insistent injunction to hurry, even though these people, like those in the antechamber of Hell, have nowhere to go. They must all the same keep on the move. At the very end of this section, however, there is a very touching allusion to Ophelia. After the sequence of 'Goonights' from the barmaid, the poem modulates suddenly into another key. 'Goonight' becomes 'Good night' (this is just like a key change where one note in the chord can be changed with remarkable effect). The final line of this section is:

Good night, ladies, good night, sweet ladies, good night, good night.

—the conclusion of Ophelia's first mad scene in *Hamlet*:

'I hope all will be well. We must be patient: but I cannot choose but weep, to think they should lay him i' the cold ground. My brother shall know of it: and so I thank you for your good counsel. Come, my coach! Good night, ladies; good night, sweet ladies; good night, good night.'

The musical effect is remarkable. By implication, in this final chord we pick up the madness and death of Ophelia, driven mad by the pressure of the world (the waste land), and driven to suicide by drowning (death by water), and thinking of burial (the corpse you planted in your garden), and her brother (You! hypocrite lecteur!—mon semblable,—mon frère!); the astonishing richness of these effects makes well worth while the searching out of these quotations, even if at first they seem a remote way of achieving poetic experiences. And it is reasonable to suppose that Eliot has the same compassion for the shadows he has so far described as Shakespeare has for Ophelia.

In Parts I and II, as well as the recognised characters, there has been a figure represented as 'I', the narrator, a man. This is the person who will 'show us fear in a handful of dust', he is the lover of the hyacinth girl, it is he who looks on London Bridge, and he who answers the first lady in *A Game of Chess*. The use of this person is in the first place a technique which allows the poet to move around among his other characters. He has no fixed personality beyond that of interlocutor and commentator. In Part III he takes on a more important identity. He becomes in a rapid sequence of quotations a mixture of personalities which eventually come together in the person of Tiresias, who is referred to in the one note of Eliot's that offers us a clue to the poet's view of the poem:

Tiresias, although a mere spectator and not indeed a 'character', is yet the most important personage in the poem, uniting all the rest.

99

Just as the one-eyed merchant, seller of currants, melts into the Phoenician Sailor, and the latter is not wholly distinct from Ferdinand Prince of Naples, so all the women are one woman, and the two sexes meet in Tiresias. What Tiresias *sees*, in fact, is the substance of the poem.

We pass at the beginning of Part III of *The Waste Land* from Ophelia's river to the Thames again, remembering that all rivers are one river, and this might just as well be one of the rivers in Dante's *Inferno*. It is another winter landscape, and one devoid of human detail, and in any case the human detail was not worth having. The narrator becomes an alloy of poets; he is Spenser, who wrote a poem in praise of marriage, *Prothalamion*, in which the refrain is the same as Eliot uses in lines 176 and 183–4:

Sweet Thames, run softly, till I end my song.

He is the psalmist (line 182) who wrote in Psalm 137:

By the waters of Babylon, there we sat down,
yea, we wept when we remembered Zion.

He is also Marvell (lines 185 and 196), who wrote a poem, *To his Coy Mistress*, in which he says:

But at my back I always hear
Time's winged chariot hurrying near.

And then he is not just these, for he is the poet now perceiving something different. The world they wrote in was not so waste perhaps as this one. The waters are not those of exile in Babylon, but those of Leman, an old word for sweetheart, a river of lovers, the nymphs and the loitering heirs of city directors, and Time is hurrying up with a macabre and ominous noise, of dry bones and chuckling. Time brings death, and a type of death in the love of Sweeney for Mrs. Porter. The Thames becomes a canal, with rats, and the smell of gasworks, and the picture is as nasty as some of those in *Poems 1920*; part of it is again the rape of Philomel by Tereus. We are still, however, in the Unreal City in winter, and the narrator has a brief encounter with the merchant, whose name, Eugenides, means well-born, but who is apparently not that, in view of his 'demotic French', his unkempt appearance, and his dubious suggestion. He recalls the waiter of *Dans le Restaurant* and looks forward to Phlebas.

Then as evening draws on, 'wakening the appetites of life in some', the narrator reveals himself as Tiresias, watching and in a sense embracing all the events and personalities of the poem, watching yet another sordid episode, in this 'world like death', between a typist and a clerk, a sexual encounter entirely devoid of purpose except as a relief to the man, perhaps; the woman engages in no more than an automatic process similar to her putting a record on the gramophone. No human feeling passes between them: 'his vanity requires no response'. And this, to Tiresias, who has seen and foreseen it all before, is the ultimate in human behaviour. If we can come up from this low point, then there is some hope, but we have to face the reality of it. We leave the typist's room and pass out into the streets again of the Unreal City, to listen now to the song of the Thames-daughters. In Wagner's *Götterdämmerung*, three Rhine-daughters lament the loss of the Rhinegold, representing the beauty of the river. Here the Thames-daughters lament a loss also, for each one has been violated, though they accept this violation with bleak resignation. The first supine, both literally and, we suspect, spiritually, the second unresenting—this is the way things are, is it not?—the third can connect nothing with nothing. She is also supine in spirit; she cannot connect 'sex' with marriage and children.

Finally, this section concludes with fragmentary references to the occasions of great spiritual importance. The fragmentary phrases refer to St. Augustine and to Buddha, both of whom speak of spiritual regeneration achieved as a result of departing from the lusts of the flesh, and adopting disciplines of spiritual purification.

It is worth remembering here, too, that on the last stage of the mountain of Purgatory, Dante encounters those who must atone for their sexual indulgence, those who have committed the Deadly Sin of Lechery. The mode of punishment is that they should be wrapped in fire for the time of their purgation.

This is the least satisfactory section of *The Waste Land*. It depends more than any other on the references and allusions, and it has less than any other a consecutive development. It is best understood in terms of the river bearing all it meets down to the sea where the death by water, the consequence of all that has gone before, occurs. The avoidance of it by the ascetic disciplines of Augustine and Buddha is by implication not taken, their teaching is reduced to fragments. The death by water is another form of purgation. (In some mythological cycles, the hero or central figure has to undergo a trial by fire and a trial by water, and this pattern is preserved here, though it is the spirit that is being tried.) The lusts are washed away entirely—the lusts of Phlebas, and of all people, because he is all of us, as the last line insists, making the identification with us, as in the first section. Helen Gardner, discussing this passage, speaks of 'its suggestion of ineffable peace, a passage backward through a dream, to a dreamless sleep in which the stain of living is washed away'.

There is a more visionary mood in Part V. If we pursue the idea of the film technique, the camera now moves more swiftly and mostly at a great distance, though occasionally it swoops in for a close-up. Even these close-ups are dream-like, though. They have not the sharp realism of the pictures in the earlier parts. It is as if we have come through to a different viewpoint, though the world is still the waste land. The verse takes on a more incantatory tone as well, fitting the new insight; the things we have seen before pass quickly now and in great profusion: faces, gardens, stony places, prison and palace, distant mountains. Then quickly we pass up into the mountains, of rock and no water, and the sensation of drought is very intense; we are almost mesmerised by the struggle over the barren rock, with the thunder beating all round, and the red sullen faces that sneer and snarl, as the vision turns towards nightmare. The verse begins to gasp in the short lines, and there is a sudden deluded moment when we almost think there is water, as we think of the water-dripping song of the hermit thrush: 'But there is no water'. The dream goes on. There are two figures and then a third, or perhaps not, for we cannot really see. This recalls the walk of the disciples to Emmaus, after the crucifixion, but before they know of the resurrection, when they see a strange third with them, who is not there when they look round to see who it is. And so there is now some hope, for Christ, as a symbol of revival, of redemption from the waste land, has entered the poem, though he is not clear to see. The vision goes on, becoming vaster in scope, with lamenting, and the movements of strange hordes over endless plains, cities breaking up and reforming, all the great cities of Europe which have lost or are losing their greatness, all the Unreal Cities. There is the weird violinist using her hair for strings, and the whistling bats, and towers upside down in the air, and voices, but still no water in the cisterns or wells.

The music of the poem is wild and exciting through this section. But then suddenly, still in the mountains, we come unexpectedly upon the goal of our journey, the chapel. It is moonlight now, and cooler perhaps, and the wind rustles the grass and blows through the derelict chapel. And the cock on the roof crows, and the lightning flashes, and then there is rain to relieve the dry land. And the thunder is no longer dry and sterile, it is now meaningful. Its sounds are represented by Sanskrit words, Da, Datta, Da, Dayadhvam, Da, Damyata, and these are interpreted as they appear. We are to give, to sympathise, to control. The giving is submission of ourselves to something outside ourselves. We stop being prudent, we stop all the things that lead to our obituaries and our wills, we cease to take account of this world, we cease to have 'the coward spirit of the man who made the great refusal'. We cease to care for ourselves. The sympathising is the means of escape from the self again, and is only another mode of the giving. If we sympathise, we enter imaginatively into another self. The control is what we have when we have come to terms with the unruly self, and have been able to subdue that which makes us self-regarding, and once this is done we achieve a kind of freedom which combines gaiety or delight with it, not the chance excitement which was Marie's freedom in the very different mountains at the beginning of the poem, as the shower of rain at the chapel was not the shower of rain in Munich which led only to sterility. We have come through the experience of the waste land, we have explored it thoroughly, we have seen the ways in which we may be made free of it, either by the discipline of the thunder, or by the ultimate discipline of the total bodily purgation of the sea. And so at last we rest, sitting on the shore, fishing, with the arid plain, the waste land, behind us. The narrator now has the knowledge, and asks whether he should respond to it. Shall he set his land in order?

The poem does not end with acceptance of what the thunder said, and the fragments at the end hint inconclusively at aspects of the experience that has been undergone. The music is brought to a close with references to earlier chords, though veiled. London Bridge, where the first crowd was, is falling down. 'Then he dived back into the fire that refines them.' This is Arnaut Daniel (see p. 95) again, on the last level of Purgatory, in the fire which burns away the burning of lust. The penitent spirits are glad of their fire, for it is not a hopeless torment, but it is a punishment none the less and so the next fragment asks 'When shall I become as the swallow?'—that is, free—and here there is a wry little echo of the myth of Tereus, Procne, and Philomela again. The last fragment, 'The Prince of Aquitaine at the ruined tower', recalls the end of the journey and the ruined chapel. A ruin, a purgatorial burning, a desire to be free, the end of a journey: this is the sequence which draws the poem to a close, and which the narrator sees as a kind of support. With these he'll fit us, and having said this he is 'mad againe', though it is a kind of mock madness, an evasion of speaking directly, a mad laugh at the end of a strenuous journey which has well nigh exhausted the traveller. It is followed by a final statement of the thunder's message, and a concluding note of peace. *Shantih*, as Eliot informs us, is the formal ending of an Upanishad, a Hindu sacred writing, and is equivalent to 'The Peace which passeth understanding'.

In my attempt to follow the overall pattern of the poem, there have been many details of this remarkably rich poem ignored, though I think that, given a pattern to work on, the reader will in due course be able to fit into it all the other implications of the imagery, the allusions, and the quotations, which I have not referred to. The poem is about the degeneracy of human nature, in particular with regard to the experience of sex and the nature of love. It concerns itself mainly with degraded forms of love; even where, by implication, it refers to finer loves, it suggests that such loves do not now occur. Its hope lies in that love which is generous and sympathetic, indeed in divine love; and the failing of the poem is perhaps in the great leap that it makes from the sordid or dispirited pictures of sexual relationships on earth to the exhortation of the thunder. At least that, one would say, was its failing if we are looking for a poem with a message. It never pretends to be that, however, and we shall get much more from it if we concentrate on the patterns of images and pictures, and on the use the poet makes of them to create a sort of rhythm of imagery, or what he would call a logic of imagery.

THE 'ARIEL POEMS' AND 'ASH WEDNESDAY', 1927–30

Among the *Ariel Poems*, *Journey of the Magi* and *Animula* are isolated poems, each treating of a single matter, and, unusually in Eliot's poetry, not closely related to the other poems of their period, except in being more obviously religious. The first re-creates the actual journey of the three wise men to Bethlehem by means of vigorous concrete imagery, and then proceeds to examine the nature of their experience there. *Animula* is concerned with the process whereby the soul of a child encounters experience, sheers off from reality, and becomes lost. Two other *Ariel Poems* belong more closely in tone with *Ash Wednesday* and form the central work of the period 1927–30. *A Song for Simeon* is a reconsideration of the story of Simeon in St. Luke's gospel (2, 25–35) from which the canticle *Nunc Dimittis* of the service of Evening Prayer is taken. Simeon has been preserved until he shall see the child Jesus, the sign of the world's redemption; he here foresees in the sign some aspects of the future, the glory and derision, the martyrdom, the ecstasy, the ultimate vision, and asks to be relieved of the stress of that experience. He foresees that the redemption offered is no easy way out. This then leads us to the experience of Eliot himself in attaining faith, which is expressed in *Ash Wednesday*, another poem like *The Waste Land* and the *Four Quartets*, which develops dramatically. During its course, a state of mind develops from one position to another, and yet the end is like the beginning:

> Teach us to care and not to care
> Teach us to sit still.

At first the poet speaks the lines as part of an effort, a discipline to discover spiritual serenity. At the end when he speaks them again it is much more with the impetus of his will behind them. The poet has given 'dramatic expression to a whole complex state of mind'.

Ash Wednesday, of all the major poems, expresses Eliot's most remote, most refined, and most personal experience. Where in the other main poems any narrator has been largely universalised, or in some way cut off from Eliot himself, this poem fairly firmly indicates its personal relation with the poet. It is concerned with the difficulty of achieving faith, and handles theological ideas in a compressed and allusive manner. Despite all this, the absolute clarity of some passages makes them most memorable and enabled the important early critic of Eliot, F. O. Matthiessen, to write:

> Of all Eliot's poems *Ash Wednesday* would have the best chance of appealing to an audience that could neither read nor write. Even though the feelings which he is expressing are extremely complex, and the sequence of his thought is by no means easy to follow, it nevertheless remains true that on its first hearing the poem is capable of making an instantaneous impression purely through the beauty of its sound. For here Eliot has been able to summon up all the resources of his auditory imagination in such a way that the listener can begin to feel the rare force of what is being communicated and to accept the poem as a kind of ritualistic chant, long before his mind is able to give any statement of its 'meaning'.

(Matthiessen's account of the poem is clear and illuminating, and his whole book remains one of the best general studies of Eliot's poetry.)

In Part I, the poet speaks of 'the Air which is now thoroughly small and dry'. His emotional experience is diminished. He has lost touch with the world, and he speaks in a small dry voice. He does not expect to recover 'The infirm glory of the positive hour'; that is, the glory of positive experience on earth giving a sense of significance. He prays to forget 'These matters that with myself I too much discuss' (Prufrock's and Gerontion's deliberations, among other things) and wishes 'to sit still', to wait on God, not to strive to understand, to turn to prayer and devotion. And yet, in the constant repetitive assertion of his present condition—'Because I do not . . . , Because I know I shall not know . . . , Because I cannot . . .'—it is possible to feel already in the verse a striving to keep this position. It is as if the poet was working through a spiritual discipline, while he is constantly driven to 'turn again'. He is attracted to the world while he tries to convince himself that his real experience of it has passed.

In Part II, he experiences the dissolution of all that produces his worldly appetites. He is dismembered, devoured, and scattered, and his clean and scattered bones sing a song of devotion to an image of purity which transcends and brings into order all the discords of worldly experience. The image is a lady in a garden. She is dressed in white, and withdrawn in contemplation. The bones too are white, and the leopards, the agents of the purification, are also white. The section ends with a further assertion of detachment from the world, and attachment to a universal principle, still and silent:

> Under a juniper-tree the bones sang, scattered and shining
> We are glad to be scattered, we did little good to each other,
> Under a tree in the cool of the day, with the blessing of sand,
> Forgetting themselves and each other, united
> In the quiet of the desert.

These are the poet's bones, but now the feeling of resistance to detachment from the world is gone. Once the idea is expressed through these images of clarity and stillness, the resistance which thinking about it brought, is dispersed. The desert is not harsh now, but quiet and reposeful, the sand is gentle and purifying, the wind listens to the song of the bones, and the song tells of the rose and the garden which unify all things, as do the desert and the wind. Finally, after achieving this sense of unity, we are led away from all such preoccupations because 'neither division nor unity matters'. 'Concentrated in purpose', in devotion to God, the bones, and hence the poet, caring for God, have ceased to care about the world, or self, and have learnt to sit still. The spirit is at rest.

The remaining sections of the poem are concerned with reconciling the two states of mind expressed in Parts I and II. While the body is not dismembered, and the bones not dried and purified, while we go on living the life of the spirit and the life of the body simultaneously, what are we to do about it? Part III takes the spirit on its journey, climbing the stair towards the goal of forcing away both hope and despair, both of which are different kinds of illusion; it practises the discipline of humility:

> Lord, I am not worthy
> Lord, I am not worthy

yet is still drawn to images of the worldly appetites. The picture seen through the fig-shaped window is intensely appealing. It distracts the spirit, which must then climb on with the strength beyond hope and despair, by faith alone, expecting neither success nor failure.

In Part IV, the discipline begins to result in a sense of redemption. The poet appeals to the lady in the garden, the same one that the bones sang of, to 'redeem the time', to signify the value of the purpose to which the poet has devoted himself. This she does:

> The silent sister veiled in white and blue
> Between the yews, behind the garden god,
> Whose flute is breathless, bent her head and signed but spoke no
> word

So she is in fact there in the garden which was so appealing in Part III and yet which had to be shunned. She is 'behind the garden god' who is 'the broad-backed figure drest in blue and green' from Part III. But Part IV ends with a reminder that even though the sign is given, we are still in exile on earth.

Part V further examines the sign. This is the Incarnate Word, the word of God revealed to the world in the person of Christ, but the Word is not to be found; it is unheard because people do not listen: 'There is not enough silence'. The revelation of God is here, but the pressures of the world draw us away from it.

Finally, in Part VI, the poet, who has now heard the Word, has seen the sign, which he had not in Parts I and III, is able to return to contemplate the world without the anxious pressure to turn from it. He is confident that in following the spiritual discipline he will be restored to unity with God. And so, although he 'does not hope to turn again', he does turn to images of worldly beauty. He is able to enjoy the experience of the senses confident that he is not in bondage to it.

This account of a remarkably complex poem does no more than introduce the barest structure of it, the movement of feeling in it. As with all Eliot's poems in several parts, what binds the parts together is only that each treats one aspect of a theme. *The Waste Land* examines the spiritual poverty of a society or civilisation. *Ash Wednesday* examines the tension between the world and the experience of the spirit and the achievement of faith. The *Four Quartets* examine the experience of time and place and the reality of experience within and without them. Through each poem there is a growth, as there is through all three taken together.

One thread in *Ash Wednesday* concerns how the poet can reconcile his intense perceptions of worldly beauty with his conviction of worldly vanity. He does so by discovering that the quickest way to the spiritual world is through the symbolic power of certain images. This is intensely developed in the *Ariel* poem *Marina* written just after *Ash Wednesday* which, together with Part II of that poem, represents the purest lyrical writing in Eliot's work. Marina is the lost daughter in Shakespeare's *Pericles*, restored at last to her father in a scene of great beauty. During the scene, Pericles is overcome with joy and hears music unheard by others present. He believes it to be the music of the spheres, the music made by the spheres of the medieval universe as they turn, celebrating the glory of God. The whole experience has been one of complete restoration of faith in divine order.

Also Marina is of a purity comparable with that of the lady in the garden in *Ash Wednesday*. Here, however, it is not the music of the spheres that the speaker hears, but the 'woodthrush singing through the fog'. The images that return to this speaker as a restoration of faith to him are those of Cape Ann, which form a strong group throughout Eliot's work. The woodthrush is in *The Waste Land* and the rocks are the Dry Salvages of the *Four Quartets*. Other images of worldly desires, gluttony, pride, sloth, lust have become insubstantial, and are replaced by subtler and gentler images: the scent of pine, the sound of water at a bow, and of the woodthrush, 'whispers and small laughter'. The speaker who has awakened to these new images realises that his boat is old and worn, and so he resigns himself to the new life 'in a world of time beyond me' which the images evoke for him, or indeed actually create for him. This is the same world of the spirit which is in *Ash Wednesday*, but here we reach it purely through images of great clarity and poignant beauty, unconnected with any of the traditional religious language. This is how the Symbolists hoped their poetry would work, and it is remarkable that Eliot has been able to achieve this conclusion using only personal symbols from his life in New England.

8

'Four Quartets'

It will be quite clear by now that the majority of Eliot's poems are not easy to interpret, for many reasons: sometimes simply his language or syntax, sometimes the form of the poems, most often the subjects and thought of the poem and the compressed manner of expression. It is said that the *Four Quartets* are the most approachable of all the major works. If this is true, it is only true in so far as many readers *feel* the poetry in the *Four Quartets* more readily than in many other works; it is not that they 'understand' the poems, for the thought behind them is as complex and as concentrated as anything we have looked at.

A particular problem arises in reading these poems, resulting from the musical analogy implicit in the title, which, although obviously vital, can lead to a blurring of effect. It can allow, as music does, the reader or listener to take from the poems whatever he chooses. He will probably notice the structure and general shape of the poems, as a listener identifies a symphony, a rhapsody, a sonata, or other musical form. He may isolate one or two particular themes or images in the way a listener will be aware of some tunes, or moments in the harmony or in the orchestration which seem to be repeated throughout the work. He may detect a particular mood, as does the listener who feels the musical work to be tragic, or joyful, or dramatic. But at that point, with the general listener to music, we have reached the limits of communication as to what the piece is about, or what it means. (There is no need here to take programme music into account, since quartets are rarely if ever programmed.) Those who listen to music know that its effect is primarily on the emotions; they know the power and variety of that effect; they know, too, that it is not to be put into words, for the words simply do not exist.

Now, it is certainly true that the *Quartets* work like music, in that they can have an emotional impact of considerable strength, while one may still remain vague about their meaning. At the same time, poetry is not music. Its effect is different, and it is different because words, as well as possessing harmony of sound, and as well as prompting both conscious and unconscious reminiscences of feeling and memory, also *mean* something; and it is in doing that, and doing it rather precisely, that poetry differs from music. For this reason, a musical interpretation of the *Quartets* is not enough.

In this chapter, I shall try to present the *Quartets* first in a rather general way, taking note of the title, and illustrating the development of the themes and the actual skeleton forms on which they are built. Then I shall treat them in a more old-fashioned way, as poems which are intended to convey particular insights and meanings. They are usually treated as a closely integrated set of poems, if not actually as one poem, which seems proper in view of the author's wishes. They are not, however, called a Quartet, which, I think, is how some people tend to think of them. Even the collective title indicates distinctions, and suggests that we shall be right in treating them as distinct poems. In addition to this, it does seem that *Burnt Norton*, which was published in 1935, and has been said to result from material left over from *Murder in the Cathedral*, differs in tone, and in content, from the other three, which were published fairly close together in March 1940, February 1941, and October 1942. The set of four was published in May 1943, in America, with no changes made to *Burnt Norton*. Finally, in this connection, there is no particular evidence of a progression through the four poems, so that although they are set in a certain order, they do not depend for effect on remaining rigidly in that order, nor even are the component parts utterly dependent on their situations in the poems. They are meaningful poems by themselves, though equally they take on further and fuller meanings in relation to each other.

Stylistically, the *Quartets* belong with *Ash Wednesday* and the poems of the period 1925–35. They are less *striking* than the earlier poems. The vocabulary and syntax are on the whole more straightforward, though this does not prevent the poet from using words like 'hebetude' and 'haruspicate' ('the formal word precise but not pedantic'). The imagery is less startling. The tone is altogether quieter and more inward, like that of a man thinking aloud, or musing, while he watches the scene at one of the places which provide the titles of the *Quartets*; it is remote and unworldly too, only returning to the precise observation of the 20th-century world on occasions for particular purposes, as in Section III of *Burnt Norton*, and more obviously in Section III of *East Coker*.

In the *Quartets* also, Eliot is far less disposed to employ the technique of literary allusion. There are occasional quotations from other works, from Dante, from Milton, and allusions to others, but none of them are prominent—a departure from his earlier method of quotation. There are perhaps three important examples, all from prose writers, and all of special significance.

The first is in *East Coker*. East Coker is the place from where Eliot's ancestor, Andrew Eliot, set out in 1667 to found the family in America. In the poem Eliot quotes a passage from another ancestor, Sir Thomas Elyot, who wrote, in 1531, *The Book of The Governor*, a famous manual on government and leadership. This poem is concerned with private aspects of time and history as they impinge most immediately on the individual. The other two important quotations of the earlier kind are in *Little Gidding*, and they are both from mystics. One is from Saint Julian of Norwich, the other from the unknown writer of *The Cloud of Unknowing*, and they mark very clearly Eliot's turning towards such thinkers to reach a solution to the central problem which the *Quartets* imply.

The *Quartets* bring together and in some ways crystallise thoughts which Eliot had been developing over the previous ten years. Several of their key phrases are to be found in earlier poems. The idea of 'the still point of the turning world' first appears in *Coriolan*. In Chorus VII of *The Rock* appears the following passage:

> Then came, at a predetermined moment, a moment in time and out
> of time,
> A moment not out of time, but in time, in what we call history:
> transecting, bisecting the world of time, a moment in time but
> not like a moment of time.
> A moment in time but time was made through that moment: for
> without the meaning there is no time, and that moment of time
> gave the meaning.

This is a reference to the Incarnation, and is very like passages in
the *Quartets*.

In *Murder in the Cathedral* are several moments which look to
the *Quartets*. Becket says to the Women of Canterbury:

> Human kind cannot bear very much reality.

—which phrase re-appears in *Burnt Norton*. The idea that Becket
must 'Fare forward to the end' is also recalled in *The Dry
Salvages*, made relevant to all of us, as indeed it is in the later
plays. A central image in *Little Gidding*, the picture of 'mid-
winter spring' at the opening, is taken up from an idea in the
play, where the First Tempter is reminding Thomas of the
delights which the earth has to offer. It is interesting to note here
that the significance of the image has quite changed. At first it is
only a picture of earthly delight:

> Spring has come in winter. Snow in the branches
> Shall float as sweet as blossoms. Ice along the ditches
> Mirror the sunlight. Love in the orchard
> Send the sap shooting. Mirth matches melancholy.

In the *Quartet* it has become symbolic of a spiritual experience,
associated with the pentecostal and purifying fire which the
dove later brings.

These are only a few of the links between the various works
of this period, but they are enough to indicate quite clearly a
close interrelationship. Each work is in some way relative to the
others and in some ways each modifies the others. This is, of
course, commonplace in all writers. The novelty in this case is
that one is conscious of Eliot's awareness and indeed employment
of it as a particular effect.

The central preoccupation of the *Four Quartets* is time. They ask the questions: what is time and how does man experience it; what is the past, the present, and the future? Further to this, what is the nature of what-might-have-been?

The next main theme is that of the relation between time and eternity, a concept which man is capable of imagining in a vague sort of way, but not of describing. It is clear that eternity is not just the time we all know prolonged into perpetuity. Yet it is not at all clear what it is, if it is not that.

The third theme is the place of man in this scheme. Man is capable of understanding things in what he regards as a unique way. Within the world of time and space he understands why things happen, but he does not understand why the world of time and space exists at all, and he does not understand why he is in it. In particular, having perceived the possibility of a supernatural cause, he does not understand why he is created with perceptions which far exceed the possibilities of the world into which he is born. He does not understand why he is born imperfect, which he all too obviously is. This is perhaps the most serious preoccupation of the *Quartets* to which the other themes are directed, though this theme is not so often present on the surface of the work.

The answers, or hints at answers, which form a fourth 'theme' are parts of a set of ideas, enlarged on in the plays. One is the necessity for acceptance and endurance. Another is the relief or release provided by divine intervention. A third is the need for purification. A further theme is that of old age, with reflections on the nature of wisdom and experience. A final theme of great importance is that of communication: the impossibility of expressing the insight which might be achieved if we had a better instrument with which to express and understand it. Each of these themes is directed towards the final optimistic assumption that:

> All shall be well and
> All manner of thing shall be well,

though I think we should be wrong in supposing that this is an end or conclusion to the poem. It is only one of the several insights to which the poems tends. In this respect it is a little like a play from which one learns about a great many facets of human behaviour, without ever really reaching a consistent and absolute interpretation of it. Such a tendency in these poems would be characteristic of an age in which most things are seen to be relative to other things.

When we turn to imagery to identify what images are used with a musical effect, we find the most prominent and memorable one is that of the garden, especially the rose-garden; and the rose in general, which tends to have to do with the experience of breaking out of the enclosing boundaries of time. It is also an experience of delight. When we enter the rose-garden, we are happy; the moment of so doing is a moment of enlightenment, which we may recognise as that at least, though we may not understand any more from it. This image is most strong in *Burnt Norton*, and is closely associated with the picture of sunlight on stone, which occurs in other poems, and in the plays, and with the laughter of children hidden in the foliage. The roses and the laughter reappear in *East Coker*, and the sunlight on the stone, though mostly only vaguely, almost as it were by chance associations. Only once does the echo become stronger—at the end of Section III when, after waiting in the dark, the soul may at last see its way out of time and into a better place, symbolised in these lines:

> Whisper of running streams, and winter lightning.
> The wild thyme unseen and the wild strawberry,
> The laughter in the garden.

In *The Dry Salvages*, the notion is first there in simple abstract terms, in Section II:

> The moments of happiness—not the sense of well-being,
> Fruition, fulfilment, security or affection,
> Or even a very good dinner, but the sudden illumination—
> We had the experience but missed the meaning,

And then very clearly in terms of the group of related images, in Section V:

116

> For most of us, there is only the unattended
> Moment, the moment in and out of time,
> The distraction fit, lost in a shaft of sunlight,
> The wild thyme unseen, or the winter lightning
> Or the waterfall, or music heard so deeply
> That it is not heard at all, . . .

There was music, too, in the shrubbery in the rose-garden at Burnt Norton. In *Little Gidding*, the memories of the rose-garden are again very slight until the final part of Section V, when brief phrases recall the set of images; and the poem draws in to a close around the all-embracing image of the rose, which now takes on its greatly wider significance, such as it has in Dante, where it is the One which embraces the Many and brings all things into order and harmony. It has been used before in this sense in *The Hollow Men* and especially in *Ash Wednesday*, Part II.

There are other sets of imagery, though they are somewhat less prominent than the rose-garden set. There is the dance, which is first 'the dance along the artery', then the dance around 'the still point', also 'the funeral dance' in *Burnt Norton*. It becomes stronger in *East Coker*, and more sinister; it is there the dance of life, Sweeney's 'birth, copulation and death', which is also a dance of death, because when you reduce life to these bare essentials, the space between birth and death becomes very insignificant. Nevertheless, the symbol begins differently in *East Coker*, for it is the wedding dance, expanded to more important status, 'a dignified and commodious sacrament'. There is then a range of earthly dancing, and a heavenly dance, which is also still—and this is one of the paradoxes of the *Quartets*. Again at the end of *East Coker* Section III, after the darkness and the waiting, as the new light begins to come clear:

> So the darkness shall be the light, and the stillness the dancing.

The image is absent from *The Dry Salvages*, though the ideas it links up with are there, but it returns briefly in *Little Gidding*, especially in the final words of the 'familiar compound ghost' whom the poet meets. He concludes:

'From wrong to wrong the exasperated spirit
　Proceeds, unless restored by that refining fire
　Where you must move in measure, like a dancer.'

The spirit, released from the bounds and bonds of time, and purified by the fire, moves on in the everlasting dance, which is at the same time everlastingly still.

A third image is that of fire, introduced already in the last quotation, and with it are associated the other three elements which were believed to make up the ancient and medieval worlds: earth, air, and water. It has been suggested, by the author, that each poem attaches itself particularly to one of the elements. It is possible to identify this attachment. *Little Gidding* is fairly clearly associated with fire, *The Dry Salvages* with water, and *East Coker* with earth, though it is not at all easy to associate *Burnt Norton* in any but the vaguest way with air. However, it is not clear what we gain from making this association. Beyond operating in a rather vague binding way, the images do not seem to add significantly to the meaning of the poem.

There are other images which run through all four poems and indeed which are present in other parts of Eliot's work. The house, for example, is prominent. So are birds. So is the sea, especially in *The Dry Salvages*, taken up from the end of *East Coker* (this is one point at which one does wonder about the relationship between the poems). So finally does the idea of darkness, of which there are two kinds: the darkness which is incomprehension and nothingness, and the darkness through which the soul must proceed before it encounters the light, which is the rose-garden. This latter darkness is derived from the writings of the mystics, who identify two states, the dark night of the body, and the dark night of the soul, through which the mystic must pass in order to achieve his desired union with the divine.

I have not in this section attempted a complete examination of the imagery of the *Quartets*, only tried to indicate lines along which it might be examined.

The structure of the poems is formal and regular, but does not in itself contribute to the effect any more than the formal organisation of any poem or piece of music, that is, in giving shape to what would otherwise lack it. In a sense, the *Four Quartets* have not the form of *The Waste Land*, where the shape and progress of the themes could be seen, whether they were made clear by any external form or not.

Each poem is made up of five sections, which correspond closely to each other in form. Section I consists of two or three parts, all of which are meditative, but one or more will be abstract while the other is more concrete. Section II is of two parts, of which the first is cast in a regular metrical form, similar to the poems of the collection *Poems 1920*, while the second is reflective and usually abstract in some way, although the themes of the two parts are closely related. Section III is also in two parts, though the arrangement and relationship vary somewhat. Section IV is always a short lyrical poem in a traditional form. Section V falls again into two, or possibly three, parts. This formal structure is something of a new effect in Eliot's writing, where in the past the form of the poems has either been very tight, as in *Poems 1920*, or rather loose. Here the poet has turned to what was earlier described as an inorganic form (pp. 45–8); there is no necessary relationship between the form and the matter.

The verse of the reflective passages is written in lines which have basically four stresses, with a greatly varying number of unstressed syllables. A ready feeling for it can be gained by listening to Eliot's recorded reading of the *Quartets* (CLP 1115), for he pays very careful attention to the versification, as he does in all his readings. The reading is, of course, illuminating in many other ways.

'Burnt Norton'

This poem opens with an evocation of our means of apprehending the passing of time, created through speculations on the nature of time. It is important to notice that we are not here reading simply thoughts about time. If that were the case, the poet would hardly have needed to devise the whole elaborate form and technique of the *Quartets*. By means of the poetry, he is trying to recreate an emotional experience equivalent to that which we have in trying to understand complex abstract concepts like time, and the past, present, and future aspects of it, including a fourth mode of time, the what-might-have-been. As we feel some frustration in trying to form a clear impression of these concepts whenever we think about them in a more than superficial way, so what is expressed here appears to be at the limits of understanding, to be moving into a region which defies expression.

Having introduced his theme, the poet turns to concrete pictures to evoke the echoes aroused by his words on time. His words 'echo thus' in our minds, in that we start to think of past experiences, experiences that never happened, and perhaps experiences that may or may not happen. His own particular echoes concern the garden of an old house called Burnt Norton in Gloucestershire which he visited in 1934, though this is very clearly only a starting-point. In the next section we are concerned with what-might-have-been, through the 'door we never opened into the rose-garden', though the images do not work simply to evoke a what-might-have-been world, but more diffusely. This is a world of innocence and pattern and order; it is also an illusion from which we must turn, not so much because it is wrong, but because it is out of time, and in a dangerous place where we become aware that reality is an unapproachable concept. We have present experience, that is all we have, and we have little idea whether it is real or not.

Section II pursues the same theme in terms of space rather than time. Space, too, is a concept which breaks down when you start to think about it. It is a complex of movement, yet movement is all relative, and we are offered a still point, the centre of the axle around which all else moves; for there must be a still point for us to be able to tell that there is movement. And as we have been out of time, so we have been out of space to that still point; but we must retreat from it, because flesh and blood can only exist in space and time. Section III examines this world of flesh and blood, and finds it severely wanting. This is a waste land picture of pointlessness and monotony, symbolised by the London tube train, a dim and meaningless antechamber of perpetual travel, neither dark nor light, inhabited by the Hollow Men. There is, however, says the poet, a kind of darkness which would release flesh and blood from this vain existence, the purifying darkness of the mystics, the discipline which will in due course succeed in detaching the disciple from the world of flesh and blood. Section IV is a lyrical expression of doubt, whether in fact we can ever expect release from this situation. Will we ever reach the still point and the heart of light which we experienced in the rose-garden? Section V seeks to answer. It suggests we shall, though most hesitantly, and finally the poem is reconciled around the fact that we had the experience; we are capable of imagining a state, a condition, now defined as Love, which is timeless and undesiring, although we could only catch it momentarily 'in a shaft of sunlight'. Nevertheless, it was meaningful, and made the prospect of time past and time future ridiculous in comparison.

'East Coker'

East Coker is a sterner examination of the way to truth, and yet in the end more hopeful. The final part of Section V is one of the moments in the *Quartets* when the reader is particularly conscious of the surge of faithful and hopeful feeling towards the right and true solution of all the problems, which is the characterising tone of the poems.

The poem begins in a more personal frame than that of *Burnt Norton*. East Coker is the village in Somerset from which the Eliot family left for America. Eliot is there, thinking again of time, feeling his way towards some understanding of it. First he imagines how space forms, dissolves, and reforms under the rule of time, symbolised in the building, crumbling, and replacing of houses. It is a hot still afternoon while he watches, and there are hints that this is like one of the moments in the rose-garden. He next imagines the passing of time in a pattern which does not change, represented by a spatial image, the wedding dance, which varies from the dignified and commodious to the ritual and animal. The rhythms of the passage move from the stately to the drum-beat. The section expresses then one of the moments when the sensitive observer may see through the boundaries of time and space ('if you do not come too close, if you do not come too close') and at the end the poet is aware of a dissolving of these concepts as they affect him. 'I am here or there, or elsewhere.' He is diffused into space. 'In my beginning' (the poem begins with an inversion of Mary, Queen of Scots's phrase), 'In my beginning is my end'. One of his beginnings is East Coker. His end, for the time being, is now. But through his imagination both these and all other 'times being' are also now.

Section II brings us in a more general way to the poet's particular 'now'. He is growing old, he is in the November of his life, and yet he is still troubled by all the surgings, all the vexations and problems which he had when young. Old age has brought no calm and peace of mind, unless it is 'hebetude'—the deliberate negation of the mind allowed to fall into torpor. The first part treats this topic by means of images; the second part discusses it, and reaches the conclusion that the only thing we learn throughout life is humility, for all other lessons are in due course contradicted or shown to be illusions or delusions. The houses and the dancers of Section I, which seemed to tell something, are gone. In Section III we are again directed away from the world of flesh and blood into the darkness, in which we must wait, with humility, to reach the light of the garden; and in the second part of the section Eliot takes up the problem of repetition. 'You say I am repeating something I have said before.' No matter. 'I shall say it again.' He then repeats a series of paradoxes, the purpose of which is to indicate a discipline whereby we may enter the darkness, which is the way to the light. Spiritual discipline is much concerned with repetition, and also much concerned with the breaking down of what seems to be wisdom and knowledge. Here is a particular case where we need to remember that we are reading a poem concerned with evoking emotional responses as well as expressing something of the experience of the spiritual life, and not just a mystical treatise.

Section IV turns at once, in another lyrical poem, to the traditional means of finding the light. The poem is a remarkably economical expression of the central doctrine of Christianity in traditional terms, though the poem uses also a range of imagery very similar in kind to that of Donne, whom Eliot much admired. The images of the surgeon for Christ, the nurse for the Church, and the hospital for the world, as well as the millionaire for Adam, are excellent examples of what in connection with Donne and other 17th-century poets are known as 'conceits', described by Eliot as 'the yoking together of two heterogeneous ideas'. Adam, who possessed Paradise, was ruined in losing it, and thereby converted the world into a hospital. To heal the world came the surgeon Christ, assisted by the nurse the Church. 'If we do well' (as much as to say 'if we are good'), then we shall 'die of the absolute paternal care'; in other words, our death will be nothing. Our means to this is through the sacrament of the Holy Communion, 'the dripping blood' and 'the bloody flesh', which is the flesh and blood of the world out of time, and is the real flesh and blood despite the fact that we think we are solid.

Section V picks up again the difficulty of communicating such experiences as these, especially at an unpropitious time (Second World War, or indeed modern civilisation which has seemed on the whole inimical to poetry and to religion) but indicates that we must keep trying. 'Old men', even, ought to be explorers. The last part of Section V brings this poem to a conclusion by restoring Mary, Queen of Scots's phrase to its proper order, 'In my end is my beginning'. As the poet moves towards death, so he moves to a beginning, and this beginning is a new end, or purpose, to his life, indicating that he has reached some conclusions; as was the case in *Burnt Norton*, he has found some shape. Here he declares it thus:

> We must be still and still moving
> Into another intensity
> For a further union, a deep communion
> Through the dark cold and the empty desolation,
> The wave cry, the wind cry, the vast waters
> Of the petrel and the porpoise.

as, to put it tritely, the river moves into and on in the sea—the image pattern to be picked up in *The Dry Salvages*.

Before this, he briefly rejects the idea at which *Burnt Norton* came to rest. The pattern becomes more complicated as we grow older:

> Not the intense moment
> Isolated, with no before and after,
> But a lifetime burning in every moment
> And not the lifetime of one man only
> But of old stones that cannot be deciphered.

The experience of the present moment with some intensity which gave meaning in *Burnt Norton* is spread, once we have the conviction which this poem hints at, and it is also shared by others at all times.

'The Dry Salvages'

The Dry Salvages—presumably Les Trois Sauvages—is a small group of rocks, with a beacon, off the north-east coast of Cape Ann, Massachusetts. *Salvages* is pronounced to rhyme with 'assuages'. This poem takes its lead from an American source, a place which Eliot would have known well in his youth. He had already written a poem called *Cape Ann*, published in 1935 and later incorporated into the series of minor poems, *Landscapes*. It is indeed a minor poem, but the group is interesting, showing again how Eliot develops a poem. As *The Hollow Men* is probably made up of pieces discarded at Ezra Pound's advice from *The Waste Land*, and as there are still two short pieces, closely associated with *The Hollow Men*, now published among the minor poems, so *Burnt Norton* originally arises from material not included in *Murder in the Cathedral*, while in this series *Landscapes* are obvious suggestions that the poems come out of the same particular creative moment. In *New Hampshire* are 'Children's voices in the orchard' which are later heard in the rose-garden. In *Virginia* is a river, still but ever moving. In *Cape Ann* we are urged, 'O quick quick quick, quick hear the song-sparrow'.

The Dry Salvages is the harshest of the *Quartets*. Its offers of relief from the human condition are slight and faint:

> Only the hardly, barely prayable
> Prayer of the one Annunciation
>
> Fare forward, voyagers
>
> These are only hints and guesses
> Hints followed by guesses

and these offers are associated with more immediately painful portrayals of that human condition than we have had since *The Hollow Men*. There remains, nevertheless, the same hopeful buoyancy of feeling in the poem as in *East Coker*, and Section V is again a great surge of feeling towards what is most strongly believed to be the right end.

Section I arises from reflections on the Mississippi, the river which flows through St. Louis where Eliot was born, and then on the sea which is 'all around us'. Both these things invade the land, where men are, and both hint at a condition different from that of men, a time which is not our time, has nothing to do with clocks, or with our ordinary mortal worries about what is going to happen tomorrow. Since both the river and the sea seem to belong to another world, both are gods, though the poet does not know much about them, even though he can identify them. The first part of Section II is as nearly tragic a piece of writing as Eliot ever writes. There is no end, no relief from the bond of time the destroyer, nor from the shipwreck of this life. The only relief, and that is both too difficult and too intense to speak of, is the announcement to man of a supernatural intervention in the form of the Incarnation. This poem is in the intricate form of a sestina, and the complexity of its rhymes reveals Eliot's remarkable command of verse techniques. The second part of Section II is similarly painful in effect. It starts from the moments of insight of the first two *Quartets*, but puts another form of rejection of them. The moments of happiness, in which 'we had the experience but missed the meaning', are no more present or significant than the 'moments of agony'. Time, which destroys, preserves also in the sense of keeping present to the awakened mind the experience of all the destruction. Then Section III leads us to the conclusion that time neither heals nor destroys for, in the passing of time, we are not there to be healed or destroyed. With the accumulation of experience, we are no longer the same person that experienced either the moment of happiness or the moment of agony. There is only one thing to do—fare forward to the only significant experience, which is death. Section IV is a simple prayer to the Virgin Mary (recalling the prayer of the Annunciation in Section II) to intercede on behalf of those who are to suffer this condition. Section V first indicates the uselessness of attempting to speculate on the past and the future, the other-worldly, like those who converse with spirits or read entrails to discover the future, such as the *haruspices* (augurers), and all the bogus people who would make contact with the other-worldly by means which are only worldly and therefore doomed to failure from the start. To apprehend the world out of time, which has been the preoccupation of these poems, is an experience given sometimes to those who are specially suited for it, by reason of such qualities as 'ardour and selflessness and self-surrender'. Most of us see no farther than 'the unattended moment' of insight, which is not, we see now, to be rejected as has seemed to be the case, which offers us hints, which we follow with guesses, and with 'prayer, observance, discipline, thought and action': a more straightforward way of expressing what in *East Coker* had to be achieved through a rather narrower and more astringent kind of discipline. What has entered this poem which is not in the other two is the idea of Incarnation, which joins the two 'spheres of existence' and releases us from the bondage. Most of us will not achieve 'right action' in this life; only the saint can do that. But we may go on trying, which will be better than giving up, and we may achieve 'the life of significant soil'—that is, a life on earth which may be meaningful.

The Dry Salvages has a different effect from the other three *Quartets*. There is a less insistent union between the concrete images and the more abstract speculations which they attempt to illuminate. Even though one attends closely to details in the sestina in Section II, such as 'the movement of pain that is painless and motionless', the poem is too immediately painful in its sense of loss and waste for us to attend very readily to its place in the pattern. This, however, is the sort of judgement which it is almost impossible to make about any part of these poems, because the pattern is as elusive as the ideas from which it is built.

'Little Gidding'

This poem is characterised by a sense of assurance: not the assurance necessarily of understanding, but of faith, of freedom from wondering. It is as if Eliot after a train of speculations similar in intensity to those of Wordsworth and Coleridge has finally reached the condition which Keats describes as Negative Capability: 'that is when man is capable of being in uncertainties, Mysteries, doubts, without any irritable reaching after fact and reason—Coleridge, for instance, would let go by a fine isolated verisimilitude caught from the Penetralium of mystery, from being incapable of remaining content with half knowledge.' Eliot himself calls this in the poem 'a condition of complete simplicity'. The pictures of which the poem is composed pass before the mind with an absolute conviction. Where in the other poems there is questioning around the nature of time, and of the timeless spiritual world, now there is relaxation:

> Here, the intersection of the timeless moment
> Is England and nowhere. Never and always.

The relaxation lies in the acceptance of the paradoxes in these two lines.

The poem opens with one of the most literally brilliant descriptions in Eliot's work, describing that kind of winter day when there is a heavy hoar frost but brilliant sunshine as well, and the cold is dry and gives an illusion of heat. This illusion is used by Eliot to express the spring of the spirit. The relation between the real spring and this spring is that between the world of time and flesh and the world of spirit. The latter is both an illusion in that it is not real spring, and real in that it is a real experience. There is no wind. The light is blinding. There is no smell. The experience is intense and pure, and awakens movement not in the body but in the soul. If this then creates the soul's spring, where and indeed what is the equivalent summer? It must be an experience of quite unparalleled brilliance and intensity, wholly inexpressible. From this experience, with awakened spirit, we look at the chapel at Little Gidding, a village in Huntingdonshire, where in 1626 Nicholas Ferrar founded a religious community, which was dissolved during the Civil War. Especially we consider the eternal spiritual significance of the place where a group of people devoted themselves to the spiritual life. We do not come as trippers, or historians, or archaeologists, but as witnesses of what happened there, whereby this particular place takes eternal significance and is the place of intersection of the timeless with time.

Section II is concerned with death. First there is a lyric poem which celebrates the breaking down of all earthly things into the four elements of the ancient world (a poetic rendering of what we know as the eventual breakdown into atoms and smaller particles). The roses of the rose-garden have withered and been burnt by the old man in the first stanza; the house and all the human aspirations and distresses it contained is now dust. Drought, flood, and fire each in their way bring things to an end. The second part describes a moving encounter between the poet and a figure made up of many influences in the poet's past, perhaps even another self to the poet. The meeting takes place during the air-raids on London in the Second World War. With death all around him, the poet hears a message of what old age has to bring from one who is dead. He may be Dante, Mallarmé, Yeats mostly, it does not matter. His message is bleak. He offers decay, futility and remorse. His means of release is through the refining fire, which is Dante's purgatorial fire, but, which is perhaps more important, it is also the fire with which the poem opened, or at least it is the refinement achieved by the spiritual discipline which has been the subject of all four *Quartets*.

Section III explains three conditions of living: attachment to the world, detachment from it, and indifference to it. This is the least clear part of *Little Gidding*, but the direction of the thinking seems to be that indifference, the Hollow Man's condition, is nothing, while either of the other two is in a sense right; and from attachment we develop to detachment. Our love of places, people, things, causes, ourselves, is a symptom of right behaviour. It is a kind of spiritual awareness fit for this world, but for this world only, and will destroy us unless we can by discipline learn to detach ourselves. We and the things we loved then reform themselves in another pattern. The poet then quotes the mystic Julian of Norwich:

> Sin is Behovely, but
> All shall be well, and
> All manner of thing shall be well.

Sin, which here means the incapacity of man to escape from that part of his life which leads to suffering, is a necessary part of the pattern, but if we undertake the discipline, assisted by the pentecostal fire, then all shall be well. The use of 'shall' is significant in implying that all *is to be* well. It is part of the pattern. The second part of Section III touches the significance of what passed at Little Gidding, and of the Civil War, and suggests that we benefit both from the victors and the losers. In the wider pattern it ceases to matter that one side won and the other lost.

Section IV is a very short lyric describing the advent of the pentecostal fire, the Holy Spirit, which is the only way to achieve release from the fire of suffering. The story behind the shirt of flame is suggestive. By way of revenge for his death, the centaur Nessus from the grave tricked Hercules' bride into weaving him a shirt soaked in centaur's blood. He said it would make Hercules love her for ever. In fact, when Hercules put the shirt on, it clung to his body, burning him with pain. He could only escape this torment by ascending a pyre and burning himself, thus escaping fire by fire. We learn too in this lyric that it is Love, or God, who devises this pattern which is unfamiliar because we do not easily see how God, in his form as Love, can originate suffering, though it is clear enough that no human love is unaccompanied by some form of suffering; and we have seen already that, in some form, attachment to persons prefigures the greater spiritual experience.

Section V presents a relaxed examination of time, and collects suggestions from all the other *Quartets*, which if we follow Eliot's thinking and feeling are with us now at the end of *Little Gidding*. Some of the problems of those *Quartets* are hinted at and seen to be of small import (though we are not indifferent to them). We are back where we started, and know the place better. In a state of complete simplicity, we accept the human condition, with humility, with sacrifice and discipline, and with the assistance of the fire and the rose united in a single image.

Conclusion

It may be thought that the *Four Quartets* offer more to the reader who believes in, or is well versed in, the Christian doctrine which lies behind them. This is not so. The presence of this feeling may stem from the necessary associations with words in English which can hardly be ignored by any user of the language. The suggestive power of words is inescapable, and its means of working scarcely controlled by the user. However, the poems must have quite as much validity, with perhaps slightly different emphases, for anyone who has some apprehension of the states of feeling and thinking that they are created out of. They do not necessarily presuppose the simple dualism of body and spirit either, though they may at times seem to do so, and then they do use this way of thinking quite simply. At times there seems to be a means whereby body and spirit merge, the world of time and the world out of time interpenetrate, not to create a mixture but to create a third state which is 'Here . . . and nowhere, never and always'. This concept is not necessarily comprehensible, but an early critic of the poems noted that Eliot was concerned with the 'creation of concepts'; and an attempt, however limited, to approach the concepts he is trying to create seems one of the best approaches to bring to the *Quartets*.

9

The Plays

In an important lecture, given at Harvard in 1951, Eliot made the following observation:

> Reviewing my critical output for the last thirty-odd years, I am surprised to find how constantly I have returned to the drama, whether by examining the work of the contemporaries of Shakespeare, or by reflecting on the possibilities of the future.
>
> ON POETRY AND POETS, p. 72

This lecture, indicating as it does the poet's long fascination with the particular problems of poetic drama and with the theatre—his first collection of essays in 1919 contains several essays on drama, one of which is entitled *The possibility of Poetic Drama*—also provides the most valuable insights into the development of Eliot as a writer of plays. It is, besides, one of the most attractive pieces of writing among his criticism, which was in the twenties rather specialised and remote, and in the thirties severe and polemical. In the later essays he became as approachable, as a person behind the writing, as he had ever been, and perhaps his last play, *The Elder Statesman*, is the most frankly personal of all his works, one of the most straightforward, though not the most powerful or memorable.

Eliot's great interest in the theatre has been in the creation of a proper idiom and form for a contemporary poetic drama. All his plays are experimental and exploratory. In the essay, he says:

> Now, I am going to venture to make some observations based on my own experience, which will lead me to comment on my intentions, failures, and partial successes, in my own plays. I do this in the belief that any explorer or experimenter in new territories may, by

131

putting on record a kind of journal of his explorations, say something of use to those who follow him into the same regions and who will perhaps go farther.

p. 78

Further to this, he acknowledges in what may appear at first to be a rather startling remark that the ideal of poetic drama is one which we can never reach, but only strive towards:

> I should not like to close without attempting to set before you, though only in dim outline, the ideal towards which poetic drama should strive. It is an unattainable ideal: and that is why it interests me, for it provides an incentive towards further experiment and exploration, beyond any goal which there is prospect of attaining.
>
> p. 86.

The whole tone of the essay, and the nature of Eliot's approach to his calling, closely reflects the peace of mind revealed in the *Four Quartets*, where 'we shall not cease from exploration' even though we have no particular hope of reaching any goal. The plays show how the poet's life draws to a gentle, patient, and temperate close both in itself and in the art it produced, with all the strenuous and disparate tensions resolved. In this, Eliot is again of the 20th century, of the age in which W. B. Yeats, perhaps the only one of his contemporaries of comparable stature, also fashioned his life's work as if it were a work of art. It is interesting that Eliot, the more remote and colder of the pair, should end on a note of warmth and intimacy in the reconciliation of Lord Claverton to the experience of this world through family love, while the passionate and burning storms which arose from Yeats should resolve themselves into the stern epitaph which concludes his final poem:

> Cast a cold eye
> On life, on death,
> Horseman, pass by.

POETIC DRAMA
Eliot's plays must be understood in the light of his intention to write poetic drama. Each, as he readily admitted, is only a partial

success, even in the face of his unattainable ideal, and he is the first to identify their failings. They are nevertheless some of the most interesting and enthralling literary 'failures' of the century, and are by no means failures if what you seek from literature is some illumination of human nature from those best equipped to examine it with the most sensitive and discriminating insight. Calling them literature, indeed, gives us a clue to their 'failure', for they are more satisfying to read than to see, chiefly because the insights they have are not such as are at all easy to come at during the course of an evening at the theatre. They are such as we would wish to think about and to return to as we make them part of our experience. At no point does Eliot achieve anything like the moment in *King Lear* (perhaps an unfair comparison) where Gloucester says:

As flies to wanton boys are we to th' gods:
They kill us for their sport.

KING LEAR IV, *1*, 36

This is a philosophical platitude, but at the point in the play when it is spoken it crystallises suddenly what we have been aware of, and takes on a refreshed vitality, because of its dramatic context. At this point, as at many others in Shakespeare's poetic dramas, the point of the union of the two, poetry and drama, becomes very clear. Eliot says that poetic drama works like music. It provides us with a special and intense kind of emotional insight working rather through the impreciseness of poetic communication than through its potential preciseness. At the moment in *King Lear* referred to, the difference between the working of poetic drama and music is clear. The poetry has created for us a kind of receptivity to such observations as Gloucester makes here, so that they emerge as moments of the greatest poetic intensity, even though the actual words are comparatively flat, and, at the same time, strike us as perfectly clear *thoughts* of some importance, thoughts which force upon us the importance of the spiritual life, the belief in a mode of experience different from, though inherent in, that of this world, and 'the primacy of the supernatural over the natural life', which is to Eliot a matter of the utmost concern. The nearest point where Eliot comes to achieving this is in *Murder in the Cathedral* (which for all his dissatisfaction with it must be regarded as his most successful play), when, after the murder of the Archbishop, the chorus utter the powerful speech revealing that they have for a moment glimpsed the deeper significance of the murder which is out of this life; but even here we are no more than in sympathy with the Women of Canterbury. Nothing in the texture of the play ruthlessly forces such an insight on us, as it is forced on us in *King Lear*.

The problem of poetic drama is twofold. It is a matter of language, and of content. It is not a kind of writing where there has been frequent success in any period in any country. The three great periods of poetic drama are those of 5th-century Greece, in the hands of Aeschylus, Sophocles, and Euripides; 16th- and early 17th-century England in the hands of Shakespeare and others; and 17th-century France in the hands of Corneille and Racine. One other successful kind of verse drama has been that of medieval England, in the miracle plays and the moralities, though there are few moments there where you can identify poetic drama. In almost every case mentioned, the chosen vehicle has been in a high style, a kind of writing which preserves an illusion of natural speech but is in fact heightened and remote, either by virtue of its rhythm or imagery or by the organisation of the words. If anything, Eliot underestimated the power of illusion, because he was at pains to refine the verse for his plays to such an extent that a natural reaction is to say that this is not verse at all, or to ask at what points are the plays poetic. He was anxious to achieve a medium whereby the audience should not be aware that it was listening to verse, yet where the rhythms and other effects of the verse should work unobtrusively to generate emotion. One of his reasons for this was that the audiences for whom he was writing were heavily acclimatised to prose drama, and would not be receptive to drama in a high style. In this he may have underestimated the living power of Shakespeare to whom the audiences were surely just as acclimatised. As he knew, he had to avoid seeming like Shakespeare in the actual verse he chose, because Shakespearean imitators had resoundingly failed all through the years since the 16th century. At the same time, once he had achieved a new-sounding verse form in *Murder in the Cathedral* it is a little surprising that he shied so far away from it in the succeeding four plays.

The other possible error of judgement in the four plays in a contemporary setting is that very setting. In choosing to write poetic dramas around experiences which would be familiar if not commonplace to his audiences, Eliot was undertaking the most startling experiment of all his works. At no period had any previous writer attempted to do anything quite like this. The Greeks wrote about mythical or legendary figures remote from their audiences, and furthermore associated with ritual and religion, in a way which must have made it easy for the audiences to accept the stylised form and presentation. The medieval dramas were also closely associated with ritual, or with experiences which the common man held to be special and set apart (also, in this case, the versification is much more obvious and popular—rather like what Eliot achieved in the special case of *Sweeney Agonistes*). The subjects of most Elizabethan and Jacobean plays are in various ways remote from the audiences. Their characters are idealised figures of the past, or they are set in foreign countries to which a mood of the exotic attaches. The French playwrights handled the most remote matter of all, going directly to the Greeks and taking over their material. Despite their aristocratic setting, Eliot's last four plays are not in any way remote, which may account for a certain uneasiness we feel in approaching such situations presented in verse.

Eliot was also influenced by more popular forms of drama. The four contemporary plays have characteristics of the farces and melodramas which were the conventional type of play attended by the theatre-going public: situation comedies, or family problems of a superficially dramatic nature, exemplified in plays by writers like Pinero, Granville-Barker, and Maugham. Their plays were not in verse, nor did they at all attempt the degree or kind of seriousness which Eliot enters into, but they wrote the kind of play which Eliot latched on to in an attempt to introduce his own kind of writing to an audience which he thought would be unreceptive.

INFLUENCE OF GREEK DRAMA

The influence of the ancient Greek playwrights on Eliot's plays is very complex and absolutely central. We have constantly seen that he is a writer who both consciously and unconsciously leans on the whole body of literature in all languages—indeed this is a central part of his belief about the nature of poetry. In the plays it is possible to identify a particular and conscious leaning on the nature and form of Greek drama in general and indeed on the subject matter of particular plays. It is the first topic which concerns us here. The relationship between the four last plays and their Greek antecedents is a special concern beyond our scope, which can be followed up in the books mentioned in the Bibliography, and, in any case, Eliot has made it clear that at least in *The Cocktail Party* he has made every effort 'to conceal the origins so well that nobody would identify them until I pointed them out myself'.

In the first part of the century, there was a surge of interest in myth and folk religion, which Eliot first attached himself to in *The Waste Land*. It was a reflection of the kind of changing intellectual milieu described in Chapter 4. It was closely followed by a review of the Greek drama in terms of ritual and religion. This identification of ritual at the centre of the earliest drama appealed very much to Eliot. He saw in it both a means of attaching his own plays to some current of feeling which might have a chance of still being part of the common experience: the human instinct for and fascination with rhythm, and equally important, a means of introducing into drama his own preoccupations with spiritual experience. Although this was in his case the precise experience of the Anglo-Catholic Church, he nevertheless wished to communicate it unobtrusively to a society where no accepted religious outlook could be assumed. One of the major preoccupations in his prose writings in the thirties was with the secularisation of society which he saw as particularly damaging, in that it was nothing; a void; not even a positive radical rethinking of human nature and society such as Communism, nor a positive acceptance of any purely materialistic way of behaviour, which in fact he would have preferred (see his essays *Religion and Literature, Modern Education and the Classics*). This was one of the reasons for his dissatisfaction with *Murder in the Cathedral*, which was all very well for those initiated into the Christian religion, and those already possessed of some awareness of spiritual experience, but which he thought would make no appeal to those who in his words 'had never thought of Christianity as anything more than an anachronism'. He is here up against a certain rigidity in his concept both of the nature of his audiences and the state of the faith he adhered to, being, I think, unduly pessimistic in both cases. It would be interesting to know his views on the cinema's large-scale religious 'epics' which, although in a sense a fearsome debasement of the higher understanding which Christianity provides of the possibility of spiritual experience, nevertheless must be evidence of a survival in popular experience of some characteristics of that belief.

THE VERSE

The verse which Eliot chose for his plays bears close relationship to that which he has used for much of his other verse works, a combination of long lines and short lines with any number of unstressed syllables and an irregular number of stressed syllables, though there are usually three or four; and in some passages in *Murder in the Cathedral* the four-stressed line becomes very assertive, strongly combined with alliteration as in Old English verse.

Eliot says that the verse in *Murder in the Cathedral* is to some extent based on that of the 15th-century morality play, *Everyman*. He says: 'an avoidance of too much iambic, some use of alliteration, and occasional unexpected rhyme helped to distinguish the versification from that of the 19th century' and indeed from that of Shakespeare. He says earlier in the essay: 'I was only aware that the essential was to avoid any echo of Shakespeare'. Professor Nevill Coghill, in his useful edition of *Murder in the Cathedral*, describes the verse of *Everyman* as follows:

Its verisification is extremely irregular. . . . The lines are of varying length and have a varying number of stresses: there is a good deal of rhyme and there are touches of alliteration. The way to feel for its rhythms is to stress the most important syllables of the most important words, and let the rest trip along the tongue, with a slight breath pause at the ends of the lines, where it may seem necessary, and a slight marking of the rhymes where they occur.

This is also a fair indication of how to feel for the rhythms and effects of Eliot's dramatic verse, though he varies from this norm a good deal towards passages full of alliteration, and to passages where there is hardly any, but where there may be other incantatory effects, such as the repetition of phrases or sentence patterns. In *Murder in the Cathedral* also he uses lines of much greater length than any in his model, though this technique drops out of the later plays after *The Family Reunion*.

Eliot himself describes the verse of the later plays. He is here describing what he arrived at for *The Family Reunion*:

My first concern was the problem of the versification, to find a rhythm close to contemporary speech, in which the stresses could be made to come wherever we should naturally put them, in uttering the particular phrase on the particular occasion. What I worked out is substantially what I have continued to employ: a line of varying length and varying number of syllables, with a caesura and three stresses. The caesura and stresses may come at different places, almost anywhere in the line; the stresses may be close together or well separated by light syllables; the only rule being that there must be one stress on one side of the caesura and two on the other.

This rather precise analysis of the verse form of the later plays is not of particular value, since it is in fact often very hard to recognise with assurance which syllables Eliot intended to be stressed. However, it does indicate the strength of his concern with this matter. His next sentence is as revealing in the opposite direction. He says: 'I soon saw that I had given my attention to versification, at the expense of plot and character'.

PLOT AND CHARACTER

As is not uncommon with writers of plays and novels, Eliot's characters and indeed the shape of his plays have a family affinity. Only a very few of the greatest dramatists and novelists succeed in putting before their readers and audiences the really distinct qualities of individuals and situations, so that there is in fact something in talking of a Jane Austen character, or a Dickensian character, or a Shavian character, whereas it is far less easy to talk of a Shakespearean character, or a George Eliot character. The characters in T. S. Eliot's plays all have a close family resemblance, even including those in *Murder in the Cathedral* (with the exception of the Chorus of the Women of Canterbury). All the characters are aristocratic, either by birth or by connection, or by association (there are important exceptions in *The Confidential Clerk*, but they do not invalidate the rule). All the characters are also sophisticated. Even when they are comparatively insensitive, they live in the smart world of country houses, cocktail parties, and psychiatrists. They are often cosmopolitan, a natural extension of that same world. And when they are sensitive, their special insights are of a rather remote and generally unfamiliar kind. These insights are the real subjects of the plays, and their complexity and profundity are perhaps a major reason why the plays are not very readily appreciable compared with some other drama. Too great a demand is made on the sheer capacity of an audience to understand what is going on in these delicate spiritual conflicts. The characters are not in themselves of that striking nature which forces itself upon an audience so that the audience may become intrigued, and to that extent involved in the play. This is one of the chief reasons for the success of plays by Bertholdt Brecht, with characters like Mother Courage, or Azdak in *The Caucasian Chalk Circle*, or by John Arden, with characters like Black Jack Musgrave in *Sergeant Musgrave's Dance*, or Johnnie Armstrong in *Armstrong's Last Good Night*. It is not altogether clear how we are to interpret these plays, just as Eliot's are at times obscure, but we are drawn towards them by the illusion that the characters mentioned have a kind of reality which we recognise as important. That is what is needed, and that is what is missing among Eliot's characters. They are altogether too cerebral, creations of the mind, unimpelled by emotions of their own. It is not that the plays lack feeling—they are shot through with all of Eliot's deepest feelings about the validity of the spiritual experience of which men are capable, and indeed of its consummate importance. It is simply that the characters take on no existence of their own except as creatures manipulated so as to illuminate and make real that experience. Eliot himself had some insight into this problem, though he did not develop it. He says of *The Family Reunion*, 'my sympathies have come to be all with the mother, who seems to me, except perhaps for the chauffeur, the only complete human being in the play'. One of the things which we may react to most frankly in *The Family Reunion* is Amy's tragedy, even though it is a much more obvious, even commonplace, situation compared with that of Harry. Amy has waited for her son to come home. She has founded her life on this hope. Now at the moment when he comes, he experiences something which teaches him that there will be no life for him at home, that he must move on to other, unknown, experience. The mother's loss, which leads rapidly to her death, is one of the most poignant situations that Eliot ever created in drama.

The family likeness is not quite so strong when it comes to plots, especially since *Murder in the Cathedral* has a completely different kind of superficial subject matter, though its real subject is very close to that of the others. In all the later four there is a sort of mystery. There is something to learn about the past of Harry, Lord Monchensey, and of his family, and it is in the clearing up of that mystery that the problem of the play resolves itself. In *The Cocktail Party*, the mystery is more immediate, but is not entirely dissimilar. There has been something unsatisfactory in the marriage of Edward and Lavinia Chamberlayne which is in need of bringing to a conclusion. This play also has the more blatantly melodramatic device of 'An Unidentified Guest'. In the last two plays we are back quite exactly with unravelling the past. Who is Colby Simpkins, the Confidential Clerk, and what skeletons are there in the cupboard of Lord Claverton, the Elder Statesman? These largely melodramatic means of attracting the audience's curiosity are quite deliberate.

They represent the first level at which the play may appeal, and may therefore be enabled to convey its deeper meaning. It is for the same reason that the last three plays are lightened by the presence of the three comic ladies, Julia Shuttlethwaite, Lady Elizabeth Mulhammer, and Mrs. Carghill, all three to some extent 'grandes dames' in the tradition of Wilde's Lady Bracknell, though much less caricatured.

The plots also have in common the characteristic that they are all family affairs. This is more meaningful. Only within the close organisation of a family is it at all naturally likely that the kind of intimate insight into human nature and the purpose of a man's life will be able to emerge in normal dramatic circumstances. Eliot has never tried to be naturalistic, nor has he ever indicated that naturalism is a satisfactory or desirable goal for a dramatist. At the same time the choice of setting for the four later plays clearly indicates that he wanted to give an illusion of naturalism, but even within the family, even though they are highly sophisticated, it does seem too unlikely that some of the conversations which are held could ever occur. The playwright asks us for too much 'suspension of disbelief', especially when he moves abruptly from a slight scene of social comedy to one of the intense philosophical dialogues between the main characters. For example, *The Cocktail Party* begins with a scene typical of cocktail parties, especially when something has gone wrong (in this case the absence of the hostess). Then, when most of the few guests who had not been put off have gone, the host is left with the unidentified guest who engages him in a complex conversation about what it means to have one's wife walk out, and further what it means to discuss such a matter with strangers. The texture is too suddenly too rich.

Another characteristic, at least of the first two society plays, is the inclusion in them of artificial supernatural elements which are peculiarly off-putting: the chorus in *The Family Reunion*, and the vestigial ritualistic actions of Agatha and Mary (as well as the part played by the Eumenides, or Furies, which Eliot soon recognised as a mistake and removed), and, in *The Cocktail Party*, the spiritual guardianship which Julia and Alec have over the other characters, despite their apparent superficiality and frivolity, and the even greater power of the psychiatrist, Sir Henry Harcourt-Reilly, who so manipulates the characters that they achieve the kind of insight into themselves that he and the other two know to be essential. He carries out the same kind of activity, in effect, as the Duke in *Measure for Measure*, who, by pretending to disappear, and then, disguised as a priest, by manipulating the other characters, brings two of them to a better understanding of themselves and their place in society. However, Duke Vincentio's device is perfectly credible at a straightforward level: he is the good duke trying to put right some wrongs among his people in the most effective way. But the three relevant characters in *The Cocktail Party* seem to have taken on their task by a divine appointment in which we are expected *a priori* to believe, and we find it hard to sympathise with what at moments appears as a self-appointed and self-righteous interference in other lives. The reason for this is that Eliot does not wish to suggest that spiritual illumination is the prerogative of either the pleasant or the sensible or even the good, by worldly standards, though I think it is true that he never makes himself very effectively clear about the kind of person who shall have this illumination. In his prose writings he refers to the presence of people in society who are more spiritually aware than others, and to their importance, and it is this sort of person who is at the centre of the plays. Quite how this works itself out in life is not very clear. This is another of the points at which the distance between the experience of the plays and the common experience is too great to make effective drama.

However, none of these criticisms diminishes the status of the plays as works of literature of great importance and great insight. Exactly what kind of literature they are is hard to define—dramatic dialogues, perhaps, directed towards an illumination of the spiritual life. As this they are infinitely absorbing. The rest of this chapter is concerned with identifying what is centrally important in each play and showing how each develops in some way from the previous one. The plays, like all Eliot's work, are intimately related to each other and to the poetry. As you read

Murder in the Cathedral and *The Family Reunion* you are aware, though not perhaps very precisely, of material from the *Four Quartets*. On close investigation, this will be found to be true of all the plays, and in the end, it will emerge that the plays are equally closely related even to the earliest poems. One of the chief preoccupations of the plays is implied in Prufrock's question 'Do I dare disturb the universe?'—the problem of right action, of responsibility. For what are we in fact responsible? How do we know what is right? Or, for these questions are altogether too 'overwhelming', how do we even begin to find out about it?

'*Murder in the Cathedral*'

This play is concerned with the nature of martyrdom, its importance both to the martyr and to his society, and indeed to the future. Eliot sees Becket's martyrdom as an action out of time, an action which only has full significance in a timeless dimension where every deed is seen to have eternal significance or eternal insignificance. Becket is one of those persons whom Eliot sees as possessing special spiritual insight and who in possessing this may be of great influence among those of his time, and, perhaps more important, for all time. Becket's martyrdom is an act of atonement for the inadequacies of this world. He is a type of Christ, who sees that for him to die is more important in the eternal dimension than for him to accept the reasonable arguments both of his tempters or of the priests. He will not put himself before the eternal order. At the same time, he must not make this sacrifice out of a desire for self-glorification. He must not 'do the right thing for the wrong reason', and this is the central action of the play, a mental action, in which Becket encounters various temptations which he conquers, leaving himself at the end of Part I in the right frame of mind to die the death ordained for him. The Fourth Tempter is the most important, the one whom Becket did not expect, who tempts him to go to his death to seek glory in the world after it, that glory which is a saint's due. He tempts Becket to die, as it were to become the Saint of Canterbury to whom the pilgrims will travel, whom the world will revere. Becket only just overcomes this dangerous insidious

143

temptation, but having done so is ready for whatever may befall. He explains martyrdom in his sermon in the Interlude. And in Part II his actual murder is enacted, followed by the curious 'justification' in which the four knights engage, when they come down from 'the high style' and address the audience more intimately in prose and with attitudes of the 20th century, an off-putting device, which Eliot faintly attributes to an influence from Shaw's *St. Joan*, where the issue of St. Joan in the 20th century is also discussed. The importance of this is to oblige the audience to consider the significance of the martyrdom of Becket to themselves, unprotected by the partition of history and verse, following as it does the splendid dramatic chorus in which the Women of Canterbury express their reaction to the same experience, a reaction chiefly of fear. They do not know what has happened, but they know it is something awe-inspiring.

One central statement in this play deserves isolation. It is Becket's first speech, which is repeated ironically back to him by the Fourth Tempter, when he himself is torn by doubts. He is here speaking of the Women of Canterbury:

> They know and do not know, what it is to act or suffer.
> They know and do not know, that action is suffering
> And suffering is action. Neither does the agent suffer
> Nor the patient act. But both are fixed
> In an eternal action, an eternal patience
> To which all must consent that it may be willed
> And which all must suffer that they may will it,
> That the pattern may subsist, for the pattern is the action
> And the suffering, that the wheel may turn and still
> Be forever still.

Becket speaks this from a position of superiority over the foolish and doubting women. When the pride of this is brought home to him by the Fourth Tempter, he cries:

> 'Can I neither act nor suffer
> Without perdition?'

and in reply the tempter returns to him his own words. This might lead us to the thought that they are untrue, or at best only partially true, since they are now in the mouth of a speaker whose powers of mind are diabolical: he is a corrupter. However, the words might be in Eliot's own manner of expression true and untrue, and in these plays we are constantly obliged to unravel paradoxes. The idea of fixity in an eternal action, an action which is both perpetually in motion and perpetually still, is none the less a central one.

Another important matter raised in this passage is the careful handling of words which is characteristic of Eliot, but not often as clearly as here, where the word patient and the word suffering are intimately related in a way which leads to various insights. To suffer something is to have it happen to you; it is also to experience distress or pain of some sort. What happens to us in this world is, generally speaking, painful (unless we have drawn a veil over any awareness of that). The word *patient* derives from the Latin word *patior, I suffer*; the patient is therefore the sufferer. He is, if he is wise, also patient, enduring hardship with fortitude. In this world we do things, and things are done to us. Both are a type of experience which we undergo, though, when we think about it, we are never very clear why we do the things we do, or why the things that happen to us happen. We know what it is that happens in the sense of being able to describe it. We do not know what it is that happens in the sense of being able to explain it. Also what happens to us and what we do are in the end the same thing, so the action is suffering, and the suffering action. This is the wheel on which we turn, and it is in essence absolute and unchanging; past and future time exist and do not exist. This is the sort of reflection that a passage of this kind in the plays provokes. A final more precise point might be to indicate that in *The Cocktail Party*, and indeed to some extent in *The Family Reunion*, the protagonists are 'patients', in the latter case of a doctor who does not signify very strongly in either the real or the spiritual action, and in the former of an extremely significant figure, the psychiatrist, whose task it is to achieve some kind of spiritual enlightenment in his 'patients'.

Murder in the Cathedral is generally regarded as the best of Eliot's plays when it comes to performance. It has a simple outline, in which although the end of the story as such is known to the audience, and no attempt is made to introduce any spurious sense of mystery here, there is nevertheless a sense of increasing tension which is eventually released in the violent chorus: 'Clean the air. Clean the sky. Wash the wind', which follows the murder. This is achieved by various means. We are not allowed to be complacent about what is going to happen just because we know all about it. Our introduction to it is through the doubts and fears of the Women of Canterbury, who set a mood of anxious expectancy. They have some inkling of what will happen and do not want it to. Then we are involved with the temptations, which are increasingly intense. Becket has expected three tempters, and combats them without undue difficulty. They represent the appeal of worldly pleasure, then of temporal power alongside the king, and temporal power in opposition to the king. Becket has foreseen and passed over these temptations. He has not, however, expected a fourth, and at this point something unexpected enters the course of events; for at first the tempter seems to be directing Thomas towards the goal which we know is to be achieved, and so we are puzzled how this can be a temptation. It emerges as the temptation to become a martyr, not in perfect humility to the will of God, but out of selfish motives to achieve the saint's earthly power, out of pride. Becket is left confused, and the doubting timorous women beseech him to save himself. Eliot has thus contrived to introduce into the play a dramatic situation in which although we know the actual outcome in terms of action, we do not now know what it means. Becket overcomes the temptation at the end of Part I, and in his sermon explains the nature of martyrdom as he now sees it. Part II is more dependent on the ritualistic effects of versification and poetry to build up a sense of climax. We wait only to see how the murder will come about. Thus, as the climax approaches, the verse becomes more and more obviously verse, with a strongly increasing use of regular and dominant rhythms and obvious rhyme, while the tension settles around the barring or unbarring of the door. After the murder, the tension is suddenly and successfully dissipated as the knights make their explanations to the 20th-century audience, leaving only the priests' comments and the final restful chorus praising God. It is not hard to see how Eliot saw verse drama as analogous to musical form, because the whole pattern of this play moves like a musical work. A theme is announced in which there is something unresolved. It is martyrdom. It has two subjects, the attitude towards it of the Women of Canterbury and of the Archbishop. Each of these subjects is examined in various ways during the course of the play until, after a climax, what was formerly doubtful is resolved, and the work concludes peacefully.

THE CONTEMPORARY PLAYS

In his last four plays, Eliot was trying to examine the same kind of spiritual issue and spiritually aware person, in a context which would make such people more immediate to his audience. All four plays involve people of special insight who, as it were, take on tasks or journeys through this world, the purpose of which is never very clear to more ordinary mortals, but is of the greatest possible importance in the eternal scheme of things. Generally we are regarded as ordinary mortals, and accordingly the precise meaning of the lives of Harry Monchensey, Celia Coplestone and Colby Simpkins is not altogether clear to us. There is, however, a brand of persons in the plays who operate somewhat between the saintly person, and the kind of person who has no insight at all into the spiritual life and who says with Violet in *The Family Reunion*: 'I do not understand a single thing that has happened'. These people are the ones who learn during the plays. Although they do not achieve very much, they are within the scheme a little bit more aware at the end of the plays than they were at the beginning. They are such as Mary in *The Family Reunion*, Edward and Lavinia in *The Cocktail Party*, Sir Claude and Lady Elizabeth in *The Confidential Clerk*, and Lord Claverton in *The Elder Statesman*. There is a fourth kind of person in these plays who has already achieved at least some kind of awareness before the play begins, though these are not of the saintly type. These are Agatha, and in a different way, Downing, in *The Family Reunion*; Julia and Alec, and again in a different rather mysterious way, Sir Henry Harcourt-Reilly in *The Cocktail Party*; more slightly, Eggerson and Mrs. Guzzard in *The Confidential Clerk*—they are less self-conscious about it. This character does not occur in *The Elder Statesman*, which is altogether the most realistic play of all. The spiritual understanding achieved by Lord Claverton is achieved not by the influence over him of any special kind of person, but simply by the unravelling of the effects and meanings of certain incidents of his past. His only assistance here comes from his daughter, Monica, who also reaches towards a new insight as the play proceeds. They learn together, unassisted by any supernatural influences except those of circumstance and coincidence.

'*The Family Reunion*'

In this play, Harry, Lord Monchensey, returns to his home, Wishwood, after a prolonged absence. He has been long awaited by his mother, who has for this occasion gathered together all the members of the family: her three younger sisters Ivy, Violet and Agatha, her brothers Gerald and Charles, and her two younger sons Arthur and John, though both of these are prevented from attending the family reunion by motor-car accidents, suggesting the breakdown of Amy's plan, which is utterly centred on herself and her life at Wishwood. She wishes 'to keep Wishwood alive', in other words to refuse to face the passing of time and the turning of the wheel which grinds human pretensions to lastingness very small. Ivy and Violet, Gerald and Charles, are wholly insensitive even to an idea such as that of Amy; they scarcely understand what is going on between the main characters, and they operate at times as a chorus, not dissimilar from the Women of Canterbury, though, unlike them, they do not achieve any real insight. Agatha, on the other hand, is much more aware of what is going on, and it is she who brings about the catastrophe, which is a clever indication of the limitations of Amy's understanding. In arranging this party to celebrate Harry's return and her triumph, Amy brings into the house the one person who knows enough of the past and of the meaning of things to convert the success to failure and the triumph to tragedy. Harry, when he arrives, is pursued by a strange force (represented as the Eumenides, the Furies, called the Kindly Ones by way of appeasement). He is searching for a solution. He looks for it at home. Agatha, who knows it is not to be found there, eventually reveals this to him so that he sees he must move on, 'fare forward to the end', as did Becket, and as we must all. What the end is, we do not know, but that does not matter.

This is the basic pattern of the play. One of its chief preoccupations is with the nature of experience and the problem of change. Eliot is concerned with these problems in all the plays, but there are differing emphases. Here we are much concerned with change. Amy resists it: Wishwood, she says, has not changed. She and most of her family cannot recognise the reality of things that have happened, not even the simple reality that one of the things that has happened is that Harry has gone away. It does not matter what has happened to him or to them while he has been away. It is just *that* he has gone away that is an aspect of the reality that all must recognise. Even if nothing had happened, which is impossible, while he had been away, he is not the same person as he was before he went. Each time we part, we introduce a circumstance which means we are not the same when we meet again: 'You all of you try to talk as if nothing had happened.' They talk like this because they are not even aware of the kind of thought described above.

> You are all people
> To whom nothing has happened, at most a continual impact
> Of external events. You have gone through life in sleep,
> Never woken to the nightmare.

Harry is trying to escape from the nightmare. He pretends, or perhaps it is true, that he has pushed his wife overboard on the journey back to England.

> One thinks to escape
> By violence, but one is still alone
> In an over-crowded desert, jostled by ghosts.
> It was only reversing the senseless direction
> For a momentary rest on the burning wheel.

He is now trying to escape another way by coming home. But he finds no solution there. He meets his past, and encounters some of the things which have been driving him on his journey, so that he feels there has been some satisfaction. 'This is like an end', he says to Agatha, who replies: 'And a beginning'—indicating that the end is but a stage in the journey.

For the reader who is prepared to encounter this play in depth, it may be the most satisfying, certainly the most intriguing, closely bound up as it is with the mood and with some of the ideas of the *Four Quartets*. Mr. Martin Browne, who worked closely with Eliot in the production of his plays, crystallises the situation:

> *The Family Reunion* is a masterpiece, but not a successful play. It can never become as popular as has *Murder in the Cathedral*. Its audience tends to greet with sympathetic relief Aunt Violet's statement:
>
> > I do not understand
> > A single thing that's happened.
>
> and Harry is continually assuring his relations that:
>
> > I would explain, but you would none of you believe it;
> > If you believed it, still you would not understand . . .
>
> For his experience is one that cannot be conveyed in words: the poet has deliberately attempted the impossible. He has thereby laid himself open to the gibes of all those who do not believe that such an experience really happens, and to the fury of people who justifiably claim that events in a play must be clear to the spectator and the story must have an end. But to those who recognize the experience he writes of, Eliot has succeeded in conveying it in this play.

It is, too, the last of his plays in which it is possible to recognise the peculiar distinctive flavour of his poetry, and his way of thinking. It is shot through with his most characteristic imagery.

'The Cocktail Party'

In this play, three figures who have already achieved the necessary special understanding take it upon themselves to bring the same understanding to others who have not reached it. They are missionaries in the dark and primitive country which is 20th-century England. One is a psychiatrist, Sir Henry Harcourt-

Reilly, whose job it is to cure people from mental disorders, and who by a simple extension also undertakes to attend to their souls—though we should beware of taking the religious imagery too far, for it is no ordinary spiritual cure that we are working towards, no common morality. He is assisted by two society figures, Julia Shuttlethwaite and Alec MacColgie Gibbs, both of whom are superficially tiresome and frivolous, but who emerge later in the play as having reached into some special fund of experience which steadily makes them more attractive.

Their patients are four other characters. Edward and Lavinia Chamberlayne are a couple whose marriage has been undertaken and carried on at a very superficial level indeed, neither even knowing what the other was really like, let alone loving. Reilly contrives a split between them, then a re-encounter which forces them to revalue their relationship, and in so doing to learn something about themselves, and about what it means to be a human being and to enter into a relationship with another human being. Their disease is that they, like most of the Monchenseys in the previous play, are people to whom nothing has happened, on the spiritual plane, which is the real one, and therefore the only one on which things can really happen. From this 'new beginning', Edward and Lavinia, like the other central figures, 'fare forward to the end'. Edward says to Lavinia at the end of the play:

> But Sir Henry has been saying,
> I think, that every moment is a fresh beginning;
> And Julia, that life is only keeping on;
> And somehow, the two ideas seem fit together.

This couple, however, represent those who can learn something about life, but who at best can only make the best of a bad job, although Harcourt-Reilly adds:

> When you find, Mr. Chamberlayne,
> The best of a bad job is all any of us make of it—
> Except of course, the saints—such as those who go
> To the sanatorium—you will forget this phrase,
> And in forgetting it will alter the condition.

The other two characters who receive the attentions of Sir Henry are Peter Quilpe, who is not ready for most of the play, but having loved Celia Coplestone, in a way, and then gone away to start his own life, returns at the end ready to undertake the higher stages of the journey; and Celia Coplestone herself, who is the 'saint'. She discovers in the hands of Sir Henry that her journey is hardly in this world at this time. It is a journey out of time which leads her in due course to a martyr's death in a remote and savage island. She, like Becket, is making atonement; like Harry too, though his is less advanced than the other two. Harry is, however, expiating a crime, though he does not know what it is, in the same way as Becket and Celia are expiating the crime which is laid on the world in the idea of Original Sin, which is part of the 'pattern which is the action And the suffering', the divine organisation. In fact, the character of Sir Henry Harcourt-Reilly is the only one in Eliot's writing which has a touch of the sort of quality which was used by Brecht and taken up by Arden, a sort of rumbustiousness, which is unworldly, and which seems to stem from a delight in finding that the world is disorderly but that it does not matter. It is characteristic of Azdak in *The Caucasian Chalk Circle*, of Wellington Blomax in *The Workhouse Donkey*, and there is a rather blackened form of it in Sergeant Musgrave himself. It is vestigial in Harcourt-Reilly, in his drinking and his song; but the song, which is engaging, is easily recognisable as a type which Brecht and Arden make full use of:

> As I was walking round and round
> And round in ev'ry quarter
> I walk'd in to a public house
> And order'd up my gin and water
> Tooriooley, Toori-iley,
> What's the matter with One-Eyed Riley?
>
> As I was drinkin' gin and water
> And me bein' the One-Eyed Riley
> Who came in but the landlord's daughter
> And she took my heart entirely
> Tooriooley etc. . . .

The singing of this song is one of the most surprising moments in the plays, though perhaps it has become so by association with the later playwrights. Nonetheless, there is something that is particularly memorable about One-Eyed Riley; he may be half-blind, but he can at least see something, where the rest of us are totally blind.

'The Confidential Clerk'

This play builds on the themes of the last, though it further develops Eliot's technique of realistic presentation, and shows him for the first time as a continuously successful comic writer. The plot of lost children and mistaken identities is too complicated to outline briefly. The central matter of the play concerns again the bringing to a greater understanding of themselves and their relationship with each other and with their children of Sir Claude and Lady Elizabeth Mulhammer. This time there is no psychiatrist for them to consult, and most of their education is brought about by the circumstance of the arrival of a new confidential clerk for Sir Edward who he thinks is his illegitimate son. Also in the household is his illegitimate daughter, Lucasta, and a man who eventually becomes her fiancé, B. Kaghan, who also turns out to be Lady Elizabeth's illegitimate son. During a series of dialogues and dualogues between these characters, with the relationships finally unravelled by a somewhat forbidding and foreboding personage called Mrs. Guzzard, who had the early charge of the two boys, and who is in fact the mother of Colby Simpkins, the new confidential clerk, all the characters learn much about what it means to be a parent and a child (this is the new emphasis in this particular play), besides learning much about themselves as people. At the end Colby discovers that it is not for him to enter into the relationships of this world, but that he, like Celia in *The Cocktail Party*, will follow the spiritual life. In some ways this is the most comprehensible play, together with *The Elder Statesman*. It is also the one with the least of the strange, special, complex effects which, however they may detract from these works as plays, nevertheless make them of the greatest interest.

This play is enlivened with a kind of personal warmth unusual in any of Eliot's writings, typified by the simple dedication to his wife, and by the subject of an elderly man finding peace of mind in the understanding of human love. This is the new theme in Eliot's last play. It is the only one in which there is no extension to take in a character of special spiritual quality, or experiences beyond the run of the normal. It is indeed an altogether simpler play than any other, and may be regarded perhaps as not much more than an epilogue of considerable charm.

In it Lord Claverton, a retired statesman of high standing, is preparing to enter a convalescent home (so-called) for what his daughter knows will be the last few months of his life. While there he is visited by two characters from his past, a man whom he made his friend, but in so doing introduced him to tastes and manners that were beyond his power of character to contain, leading to his eventual downfall, in England at least; and a woman whom he once loved, but did not marry, and who sued him for breach of promise. These two force upon him an examination of his life, particularly with regard to his responsibility for his son, who is weak and feckless. When Michael, the son, comes to him to ask for help to leave England and start another career, Lord Claverton cannot extend his sights so far yet. He wishes to keep the boy under his control, to avoid in him the mistakes of his own youth. But he does soon at least see this much:

> What I want to escape from
> Is myself, is the past. But what a coward I am,
> To talk of escaping! And what a hypocrite!
> A few minutes ago I was pleading with Michael
> Not to try to escape from his own past failures:
> I said I knew from experience. Do I understand the meaning
> Of the lesson I would teach? Come, I'll start to learn again.
> Michael and I shall go to school together.

In the third act, the two people from his father's past offer Michael a new start in a job abroad which he wants and which his father now sees he cannot and indeed should not prevent, despite the rather harsh irony in the fact that it is these two who are doing it. He has disclosed their significance to his daughter, who has forgiven him for whatever he may need forgiveness for, and having come to terms with the past and with his son, Lord Claverton is at peace:

> This may surprise you: I feel at peace now.
> It is the peace that ensues upon contrition
> When contrition ensues upon knowledge of the truth.
> Why did I always want to dominate my children?
> Why did I mark out a narrow path for Michael?
> Because I wanted to perpetuate myself in him.
> Why did I want to keep you to myself, Monica?
> Because I wanted you to give your life to adoring
> The man that I pretended to myself I was,
> So that I could believe in my own pretences.
> I've only just now had the illumination
> Of knowing what love is. We all think we know
> But how few of us do! And now I feel happy—
> In spite of everything, in defiance of reason,
> I have been brushed by the wing of happiness.
> And I am happy, Monica, that you have found a man
> Whom you can love for the man he really is.

This passage contains several of the most important ideas of Eliot's later work, and indicates where his thoughts have tended to fall: 'knowledge of the truth'.

He has sought all his life for this with the greatest possible astringency. The avoidance of pretence, the identification of love, the identification of what a man is, each of these mark out the direction of Eliot's search. This play especially finds its solution in the discovery of a true love within the family, which has been earlier expressed, or not expressed, by Monica:

> You know that I would give my life for you.
> Oh, how silly that phrase sounds! But there's no vocabulary
> For love within a family, love that's lived in
> But not looked at, love within the light of which
> All else is seen, the love within which
> All other love finds speech.
> This love is silent.

Here too it becomes clear why Eliot has been in his last four plays preoccupied with family situations. The love which he is describing here is human and divine. It is small and intimate, and it is vast and all-embracing. It is the love which has created the pattern of action and suffering. Monica finds her other love in her future husband Charles, of which love she says:

I've loved you from the beginning of the world.
Before you and I were born, the love was always there
That brought us together.

Here at last is an action taken, a situation entered into with certainty and responsibility in the knowledge that the universe will not be disturbed.

Postscript

'Sweeney Agonistes'

Eliot's first excursion into drama was in 1926-7 in the fragments of *Sweeney Agonistes*, which are a tailpiece to much that was in the first books of poems, but which are also an indication of what Eliot will be preoccupied with in handling drama. They continue the cosmopolitan atmosphere of the early poems, picking up certain characters from those. They imply the same kind of tired, bored, desiccated, fragmented world which has been Eliot's whole preoccupation. And we can learn just enough from them to see that Sweeney has by this time become the central figure, the one whom the rest will not understand, who has the special awareness. In the second fragment, when he is trying to explain an important experience involving a murder, he says 'But I've gotta use words when I talk to you'—referring to the impossibility of communicating the heart of the experience to others who have gone through nothing like it.

The main interest of the piece is in its style, however, for in reaching towards a verse form, here Eliot employs very strong rhythms, usually described as jazz rhythms, because the same phrases are repeated but with the stresses moved about. Also the pieces have several songs in them, and Eliot has suggested that much of the verse should be accompanied with drumbeats, so that the whole must take on more obviously a ritualistic flavour. A splendid insight into the possibilities of these fragments is provided on record CLP 1924. This is a recording of a memorial programme to T. S. Eliot performed in 1965. The vitality of the dialogue, and the appropriateness of the lyrics for the songs is immediately apparent, especially also the adaptability of the lyrics to renderings in the current popular manner, not specially that of the twenties. The fragments are also completed by a curious piece of near-nonsense writing, which is not published in the *Collected Poems*, though it appears in Carol H. Smith's book mentioned in the Bibliography. She also provides a very interesting and detailed analysis of these pieces.

Bibliography

This book list does not attempt to be comprehensive, but is meant to be used in conjunction with various chapters in this study of T. S. Eliot, as further reading:

HIS LIFE

T. S. Eliot. A Symposium for his Sixtieth Birthday, edited by Tambimuttu and Richard March (Cass, 1948. Third impression, 1965).

T. S. Eliot, the Man and his Work, edited by Allen Tate (Chatto and Windus, 1967).

Hugh Kenner: *The Invisible Poet* (University PB, Methuen, 1965).

Herbert Howarth: *Notes on Some Figures behind T. S. Eliot* (Chatto and Windus, 1965).

Charles Norman: *Ezra Pound* (Collier-Macmillan, 1960).

HIS POETRY

F. O. Matthiessen: *The Achievement of T. S. Eliot* (Galaxy Books, New York: Oxford, 1958).

Helen Gardner: *The Art of T. S. Eliot* (The Cresset Press, 1949).

These two are among many critical books on all features of Eliot's poetry, but for full explanatory details of the meanings of the poems the following are most helpful:

George Williamson: *A Reader's Guide to T. S. Eliot* (Thames and Hudson, 1955).

Grover Smith: *T. S. Eliot's Poetry and Plays* (Phoenix Books, University of Chicago Press, 1956).

GENERAL CRITICISMS OF MODERN POETRY

Edmund Wilson: *Axel's Castle* (Fontana, Collins, 1961).

F. R. Leavis: *New Bearings in English Poetry* (Chatto and Windus, 1950).

GENERAL LITERARY BACKGROUND

V. De S. Pinto: *Crisis in English Poetry, 1880–1940* (University Library, Hutchinson, 1955).

Enid Starkie: *From Gautier to Eliot* (University Library, Hutchinson, 1962).

HIS PLAYS

D. E. Jones: *The Plays of T. S. Eliot* (Routledge, 1960).

Carol H. Smith: *T. S. Eliot's Dramatic Theory and Practice* (Oxford, 1963).

Both these two books discuss Eliot's plays in detail and they also have many references to other critical studies and articles. The following are helpful too:

Murder in the Cathedral, edited by Nevill Coghill (1965), has a particularly clear and useful introduction to the play.

Raymond Williams: *Drama from Ibsen to Eliot* (Penguin PB, 1964) sets the playwright in a wider context.

GRAMOPHONE RECORDS OF HIS WORK

Memorial Record of Homage to T. S. Eliot (includes a performance of *Sweeney Agonistes*): E.M.I. CLP 1924.

T. S. Eliot reading poems and choruses (includes *Prufrock*, *Ash Wednesday*, and *Marina*, among others): Caedman Literary Series: TC 1045.

The Caedman Treasury of Modern Poets (*The Waste Land*): Caedman: TC 0994.

Four Quartets read by the author: E.M.I. CLP 1115.

Index to the works of T. S. Eliot